SO YOU
THINK YOU
CAN THINK

Thinking through moral
dilemmas in pursuit of justice

OTTO B. TOEWS, PH. D.

 FriesenPress

Suite 300 - 990 Fort St
Victoria, BC, V8V 3K2
Canada

www.friesenpress.com

ISBN
978-1-5255-0539-3 (Hardcover)
978-1-5255-0540-9 (Paperback)
978-1-5255-0541-6 (eBook)

1. PHILOSOPHY, ETHICS & MORAL PHILOSOPHY

Distributed to the trade by The Ingram Book Company

Dedicated to:

Joan McCreath, my wife, for your support and tireless editing.

Konrad, my son, chef and musician, died February 14, 2015.

Eleanor (MBA), my daughter, who works and travels worldwide.

Table of Contents

Part II

Part IV

Reference

Acknowledgements

End Notes

Figures

Preface

"I have collected coins for many years and stored them in this jar," said Grandma to two of her pre-school-aged grandsons. "Most of them are pennies from many years ago. I would like you to have the pennies." With that she poured the coins onto the kitchen table - lots of them. The two brothers exclaimed "Yes!" at the same time and dove into the pile of coins. Each made a pile of pennies. The older brother, Tommy, ended up with a much bigger pile.

"Can you share the pennies so that you both have the same number of pennies to take home?" asked Grandma. At that moment, Billy, the younger brother, shouted, "Give me some pennies! You have more than I have!"

Said Grandma to Tommy, "Well, can you share some of your pennies with your brother?"

To her surprise, Tommy exclaimed, "No! These are my pennies ... I found them."

Grandma asked again, "Tommy, could you please share some of your pennies with Billy? Then both of you would have the same number of pennies." But to no avail. Tommy wrapped his arms around his pile of pennies and insisted on keeping all of them.

Grandma had created a problem with her offer; she had forgotten for a moment that at the pre-school age, children sometimes have difficulty with the notion of fairness. Does that sound familiar to you?

Now look at this scenario which happened in a Grade 7-9 junior high school. A few minutes after the lunch break, two eighth grade boys, Peter and Jack, were sent to the principal's office. They had been involved in a brief scuffle in the gym. Jack had fallen to the floor and, for good measure, Peter had kicked Jack in the head.

Before the principal could ask some questions about the incident, Peter, the boy who kicked Jack in the head blustered, "He started the fight ... I was just defending myself. You [pointing to Jack] would have done the same to me!"

"I have never done anything like that to you or anyone else!" retorted Jack. "I could have suffered a concussion; then you would've been sorry. Kicking someone in the head is an act of violence! It's wrong!"

Finally, the principal got a word in edgewise and asked, "What's the right thing to do going forward?"

"Kick Peter out of our school," Jack fired back, "and make him apologize to me."

"That's not fair," insisted Peter. "I could lose a whole year of school."

"Would serve you right," Jack retorted with a sneer.

It was obvious that the boys would not be able to resolve this problem between them.

Did you notice how the two scenarios are different from each other? When Tommy was asked to share some of his pennies with his brother, he simply tried to protect his pennies by wrapping his arms around them. No arguments ... only control. On the other hand, Peter immediately defended his actions by placing the blame on Jack. It's interesting that Peter did a role exchange in his defence by reversing their roles, "You would have done the same to me!" Jack argued that what Peter did was wrong; he called it a form of violence. Both took a personal perspective on the question the principal asked, "What's the right thing to do going forward?" This exchange reflects a more complex way of thinking about what happened compared to Tommy's reaction. Peter and Jack attempted to give reasons for their respective positions. Peter even did a role exchange in his own defence. Both cases included moral dilemmas in that they involved conflicts of interest. Grandma asked Tommy to share some of his pennies with Billy; Tommy didn't want to. Peter and Jack could not agree on what would be the right punishment for Jack. I call them moral dilemmas because they involved issues of right and wrong.

Of course, we assume that adults think through moral dilemmas much more thoroughly. However, I refer you to a study conducted in 2008 by sociologist Christian Smith and reviewed by David Brooks, a columnist for the *New York Times*[1]. The young people in the study, when asked to describe a moral dilemma they had faced, came back time and again saying, "It's up to the individual. Who am I to say?" They agreed that rape and murder are wrong. But moral thinking didn't enter the picture for them, even when they considered issues like drunk driving, cheating in school or cheating on a partner. They did not express any intent to do the right thing because it is the right thing to do. They did not consider whether they were obliged to do their duty for some particular reason. They did not consider whether they ought to do the right thing if they were in a position to do it.

This led Brooks to conclude that people need ways of thinking through moral dilemmas as they face issues like cheating. I agree with Brooks. Hence, the goal of the first part of the book addresses this challenge: *Thinking through moral dilemmas to resolve them in pursuit of justice or fairness.* To that end, I present a Principled Thinking Model which addresses five basic issues involved in resolving moral dilemmas in a just and fair way. They are:

- Act from a desire to do one's *duty*
- Recognize a person's *rights*
- Act from a morally good *motive*
- Give people what they *deserve*
- Act with impartiality in pursuit of *justice*

Since these questions focus on resolving moral dilemmas, more clarification is needed. *Moral dilemma* refers to situations where people face a conflict of interest. Tommy experienced a conflict of interest when he was asked to share some of his pennies with Billy. Peter and Jack experienced a conflict of interest. Jack insisted that Peter receive severe punishment; Peter objected claiming that expulsion would be unfair. The principal would have to help the two boys resolve the conflict in a just and fair way.

Thought experiments are used throughout the book to describe ways of resolving moral dilemmas. They are applied to hypothetical scenarios to demonstrate the application of the Principled Thinking Model.

Let me explain thought experiments by comparing them to empirical experiments based on collecting relevant information. First, let's review empirical experiments. In the Introduction, I defend the students' use of thinking strategies when they write essays by reporting on the outcomes of a ten year study on the use of thinking strategies. The research teams assessed the performance of the students who used specific thinking strategies. The assessments showed that the students' performance improved significantly when they used thinking strategies as they wrote essays and reports. In Part I, I point out that Lawrence Kohlberg defended stages of cognitive development by conducting repeated cross cultural studies. These studies were used to validate the theory that people go through invariant stages of cognitive development. In short, both studies focused on validation based on relevant information or data.

Thought experiments, on the other hand, do not rely as exclusively on collecting performance information, but rely more on thinking through problems or issues. Paul Thagard, professor of Philosophy and director of the cognitive science program at the University of Waterloo, describes thought experiments as a "mental construction of an imaginary situation in the absence of attempts to make observations of the world."[2] It is used widely by scientists and philosophers. Let me illustrate how they are used by Nassim Nicholas Taleb[3], a philosophical essayist and academic researcher at New York University's Polytechnic Institute, and John Rawls, professor of Philosophy at Harvard University.

Nassim Nicholas Taleb used thought experiments in *The Black Swan* to address the puzzle of the Black Swan. Whereas empirical experiments focus on the expected, Taleb's Black Swan is focused on the unexpected. It is focused more on what we don't know than on what we know. By way of an example, Taleb refers to the terrorist attack on September 11, 2001 in New York. Had this attack been conceivable on September 10, it would not have happened. In other words, had the authorities engaged in a thought experiment on the possibility that terrorists might plan to cause damage to the United States by flying planes into the twin towers in New York, no doubt the US would have taken steps to prevent it. This decision would not have been made on the basis of new information but through a thought experiment which could have prevented the terrorist attack. Only after the attack, did pundits and politicians attempt to make it explainable or predictable based on new information, namely, that an attack had occurred.

John Rawls used thought experiments in *Theory of Justice* to explain the concept of *justice* as it relates to resolving moral dilemmas. He developed a theory of justice base on the traditional theory of social contract and contrasted it to the prevailing theory of utilitarianism. He maintained that his concept of justice provides a more adequate moral basis for a democratic society grounded in liberty and equality. Rawls does not defend his position based on empirical evidence but on an analysis of two competing concepts: social contract and utilitarianism. He used thought experiments to present his position on 'justice' based on his understanding of social contract.

Thought experiments are applied in this book in an ongoing conversation between two teachers, Mae and Bill, who discuss what the categories of the Principled Thinking Model mean to them. They engage in discussing mostly educational issues related to students and parents. For example, look at their discussion about duty:

> Immediately they disagreed on whether all references to duty raise moral issues. Bill asserted, "Every reference to duties involves a moral sense. Any reference to doing one's duty is about right and wrong action."
>
> "Not so quick," said Mae. "The term *wrong* is used in the moral sense in, 'It is wrong for children to pick on the new classmate.' On the other hand, the term is used in a non-moral sense in, 'He gave the wrong answer to that math question."
>
> Bill had to concede to this distinction. At the same time, he added, "If it is a person's duty to do something, then the act of doing it is morally right and it would be wrong not to do it."
>
> "Before we get too far into our conversation about duty, we need to be clear about what is meant by doing one's duty," cautioned Mae.

"That's easy," retorted Bill. "It simply means a person follows whatever is his duty to do. Typically, people simply follow whatever duty has been assigned to them. For example, when I have been assigned to lunch hour hallway supervision by my principal, I do it. No questions asked. Most teachers I know would do the same."

"Really?" asked Mae. "Does it not matter whether a person actually wants to do what is his duty to do? Does it matter to you whether you personally want to do what you have been assigned to do?"

"Well, maybe," admitted Bill.

"And," Mae added, "what if someone wants to do his duty *only* if it's the right thing to do?"

Bill had to concede again. He had been too quick to accept a simple meaning of wanting to do one's duty.

In their later conversation, Mae and Bill move on to discuss controversial issues such as cyber bullying and reconciliation not from a strictly legal point of view but from a moral point of view. For example, when Mae and Bill discuss reconciliation in Chapter 21, Mae says, "It probably includes a reciprocal relationship between the one-caring and the one-cared-for. Both parties need to support each other. That might be a promising path towards reconciliation."

The Principled Thinking Model presented in this book does not guarantee right answers but serves as a way of thinking through different situations involving moral dilemmas. Thought experiments are used to present and defend that process.

That's why this book is titled: *So You Think You can Think: Thinking through moral dilemmas in pursuit of justice.* This book encourages us to re-examine our perceptions and decisions regarding morality so that we are better prepared to act accordingly. Thought experiments offer one way of doing that.

I conclude that, while thinking through moral dilemmas is necessary for resolving moral dilemmas in pursuit of justice or fairness, more is needed. Let me explain. If Tommy had felt that it was unfair that his brother had fewer pennies, he might have shared some of his pennies with his brother. Tommy felt no empathy for Billy; hence he didn't feel badly for not sharing his pennies with Billy; only his own interests mattered.

As for Peter, he justified his action by blaming Jack and assuming no responsibility for his action. He even used role reversal to defend himself. He maintained that Jack would have done the same thing. Had he felt empathy for the injury he caused Jack, he might have offered an apology; he showed no sense of fellow-feeling or empathy for Jack.

The young people in a 2008 study reviewed by Brooks did not think through the rights and duties to resolve issues such as cheating. They took a purely personal approach to these issues. No consideration was given to other people's feelings ... just their own. No thought was given to anyone's rights or duties.

This raises the second major point made in this book: *Resolving moral dilemmas in pursuit of justice requires a sense of fellow feeling or empathy, as well as thinking through moral dilemmas.*

I recommend that developing such empathy can be accomplished by applying Kurt Baier's[4] four moral values principle tests:

New Cases Test - consider a tentative value decision in similar new cases.

Role Exchange Test - encourage people to apply a value decision to themselves before prescribing it for others.

Subsumption Test - explore the interrelationship of principles by prioritizing competing principles.

Universal Consequences Test - consider the consequences of applying a decision to all like hypothetical or real situations.

For example, the Role Exchange Test involves putting oneself in the shoes of another person to experience their point of view. If Jack would have put himself in Peter's position, he might have offered a less severe form of punishment for Peter. These tests evoke a sense of fellow-feeling that is needed for people to think through moral dilemmas in pursuit of justice or fairness.

Look at the following exchange between Mae and Bill about *motive* which is another category along with rights and duty in the Principled Thinking Model:

Out of nowhere, Mae added, "I think that morally good motives and empathy need to go together! It's ridiculous to separate them and suggest that empathy has a lesser role to play in moral action. In fact, what could possibly drive a person to action more than the emotional energy of empathy?"

Before Bill could respond, Mae continued, "What is more likely to drive a young person to assist an older person to cross a busy street safely? Would it be a cold calculated assessment of the likelihood that the older person might get hit by a car as he stumbles across the street? Or, might a young person feel a sense of concern, even empathy, for the older person while he considers the risk of allowing the older person cross the street by himself? In fact, I am convinced that both, thinking and empathy, are needed for people to act on morally good motives."

"WOW," Bill muttered. "I never thought of it that way. Maybe we need to consider both. Thanks, Mae."

This had indeed been a Eureka moment for both of them. Would this discovery change their conversation about justice or fairness? Only time will tell.

The core of this book explores the power of using categories and concepts to think through moral dilemmas in pursuit of justice or fairness. However, I acknowledge the need for a sense of empathy or fellow feeling as a necessary foundation for resolving moral dilemmas. Without the urgency and energy generated by a sense of caring or empathy, thinking through moral dilemmas, while necessary, is insufficient for pursuing justice or fairness.

Introduction

Writing the book, SO YOU THINK YOU CAN THINK, was preceded by several years of teaching history where I coached students to write persuasive essays. They were challenged to think critically about their ideas as they wrote. For example, I would ask students to write an essay on a topic like: The Barons in 1066 had a right to confront their king, King John, about his abuse of his powers. Agree or disagree by defending or challenging the Baron's rights. To respond to this question, the students had to think critically about King John's rights and responsibilities as well as the Baron's rights and responsibilities in a time when they had no legal right to challenge the King. Consequently, the students did very well on externally set government exams, which required them to write essays. Still I was curious as to whether these positive results were due, in part, to the focus on thinking I had encouraged. As I explain below, studies, which I conducted years later, showed a positive correlation between introducing students to a variety of thinking strategies and the quality of their essays. The Studies and thinking strategies are posted on my website, www.sponsoravillage.ca[5].

I interrupted my teaching career by engaging in two years of graduate studies in philosophy and theology. This led me to a deeper appreciation of the value and importance of relationships people share; nurturing mutual relationships became the foundation of morality for me.

My return to teaching history was interrupted again because I was curious about how adolescents think through controversial issues. Consequently, I explored the cognitive development of adolescents in a Masters[6] program under the leadership of Professor Terry Morrison, focusing on Lawrence Kohlberg's[7] stages of cognitive development and the psychological and philosophical framework he developed. These studies prompted me to conduct a ten years Study *Writing for Meaning*[8] which focused on the impact of challenging adolescents *to think as you write and write as you think.*

To support this study on thinking and writing, my colleague, Dr. Robert Cross, and I developed software, *writer's*KnowledgeBuilder[9], using a research grant from Apple Canada to facilitate the writing and editing process. This platform was used in the ten year study, *Writing for Meaning*, to support students in revising and editing their essays. In follow-up questionnaires, students maintained that the platform assisted them with revising and editing their essays.

We followed up with the development of a multimedia-authoring platform, *multimedia*KnowledgeBuilder[10], to enable students to express themselves through multiple mediums. This platform provided students with an integrated environment where they could move seamlessly from expressing their thoughts and arguments through text, audio, pictures, hyperlinks, and videos. This software also included a wide range of thinking and writing strategies to prompt students to consider and use different ways of presenting their knowledge.

To demonstrate how this software could be used to create dynamic interactive stories, I created a CD, *In Pursuit of Justice*[11], where users can navigate through a huge body of resources on the history of Japanese Canadians including text, audio, pictures, hyperlinks and videos. Students could download the CD and add new resources to it, thus, expanding the story. They were encouraged to use this platform as they were writing stories, essays and reports.

However, a big question still remained for me: Does a focus on thinking lead to adolescents' ability to think through controversial issues? Hence, I launched a ten year study, *Writing for Meaning*, to determine the effect of introducing students to a range of thinking strategies on their ability to write persuasive essays. The assessment of *Writing for Meaning* was conducted by third party using pre- and post testing of pilot and control groups. The results of these assessments confirmed the power of using thinking strategies in writing essays. The performance of the students in the pilot groups was significantly higher than the performance of the students in the control groups. The students in the pilot groups also consistently performed significantly higher on post tests as compared to their performance on their pre-tests.

Alison Armstrong, an author of several books and contributor to *The Toronto Star* and *The Globe and Mail*, visited some of the schools involved in the studies and reviewed several assessment reports. She concluded in the book *the child and the Machine* (co-authored with Charles Casement, a freelance writer and editor in the field of education in England and Canada) that, based on the studies, "There was significant improvement in the thinking and writing skills of the students involved."[12]

The results of these studies were exciting and generated more questions. Specifically, they raised the question, "What categories and concepts do people need to resolve moral issues through critical thinking?" In other words, is there a set of interrelated words or groups of words that address this question? For example, the concepts of paper, laptop, keyboard, pencil, desk, and chair all can be grouped under the category of writing. Is there a similar list for thinking through moral issues?

Another sabbatical and the pursuit of studies in moral philosophy (in a Ph, D. program) enabled me to address this question. The emerging Principled Thinking Model, which serves as the core of this book, had its origin in a graduate Philosophy course taught by Professor Peter Glassen at the University of Manitoba and in a series of articles[13] he wrote. In the year-long seminar, Professor Glassen challenged his class to explore a range of categories and concepts for thinking through moral dilemmas. The categories were: duty, rights, motive, desert and justice. They served as the basis for the Normative Conceptual Framework for exercising discretion in making moral decisions which I developed in my doctoral dissertation under the direction of Professor Anthony Riffel. This framework became the basis for the Principled Thinking Model for this book.

As principal of a school, I had many opportunities to use the framework in working with students to resolve conflicts that arose between them. The story in the Preface involving Peter and Jack is one example. It was also interesting to observe how students in my university graduate classes responded to using my model for resolving conflicts.

However, I was still left with the nagging questions: "Is morality strictly a cognitive exercise? Are there no emotions involved that drive moral action?" The need for something more became abundantly evident as I applied the framework in working with students to resolve everyday conflicts. In my subsequent search, I discovered Kurt Baier's Moral Values Principle Tests, which appeal to the emotional side of moral action. As I mentioned in the Preface, Baier developed four tests: New Cases Test, Role Exchange Test, Subsumption Test, and Universal Consequences Test. They became an integral part of the process of helping students resolve conflicts.

Let me illustrate briefly how these tests can be applied using the scenarios in the Preface. If Tommy could have put himself in Billy's shoes (the Role Exchange Test), would he still have insisted on not sharing his extra pennies with Billy? Apparently, he could not empathize and so he kept all the pennies to himself. Peter presented a new case (New Cases Test) where Jack would have kicked Peter in the head, but, he did not change his view about being innocent. Would Peter have come to the same conclusion if he had considered the universal consequences of his action (Universal Consequences Test) which poses the following question: "What if people always defended their wrong action and refused to take responsibility for their own action?"

I need to caution against the tempting conclusion that an appeal to the emotion of empathy is sufficient for resolving moral dilemmas. Lawrence Kohlberg describes this claim as a romantic ideology, which assumes "what comes from within the child is the most important aspect of development."[14]. Children's learning environment should be permissive enough to allow the inner *good* to unfold and for the inner *bad* to come under control reflecting natural development. Brooks maintains that the young people in the Study by sociologist Christian Smith[15], insisted that in virtually all situations, whether an act is right or wrong, is up to the individual. The only exceptions for them were rape and murder. Brooks elaborates on the views of young people in *The Road to Character*[16] published in 2015, as a subjective view. In my book, I pose this as an alternative to applying the Principled Thinking Model and the Moral Values Principle Tests.

I conclude that the Moral Values Principle Tests together with the Principled Thinking Model enable us to resolve moral dilemmas in pursuit of justice or fairness by applying them to a number of scenarios. At the same time, I recognize that they do not guarantee morally right answers because the tests and the model together reflect a process and not correct universal answers.

This is how the book is organized.

Part I: Thinking through moral dilemmas to resolve them in pursuit of justice or fairness

Chapter 1: Challenge provides a brief context for the thinking necessary to resolve moral dilemmas. Two cases are presented to illustrate the need for categories and concepts to make right and wrong decisions. The first case, as presented by David Brooks, addresses the need of young people for categories to resolve moral dilemmas. The second case presents the challenge of using artificial intelligence in driverless cars.

Chapter 2: Cognitive development is based on the work of Jean Piaget[17] and Lawrence Kohlberg who explain how people can develop increasingly more differentiated and integrated forms of thought to resolve moral dilemmas. According to Kohlberg, at Stage 1 children try to avoid punishment by being obedient to authorities. At Stage 2 children reflect a primary concern for their own needs and do not distinguish between the value of life and property. At Stage 3 children focus on good behavior which helps others and is approved by them. At Stage 4 young people are aware of social order and concerned about maintaining it through rules and in doing their duty. At Stage 5 people focus on social utility. Finally, at Stage 6 people act on the basis of self-chosen ethical principles grounded in logical consistency and universality.

Chapter 3: Effortful reasoning distinguishes System 1 from System 2 thinking. System 1 thinking refers to fast or intuitive thinking which depends on heuristics, perception and memory. It refers to the instant responses we make in spontaneous situations or acts. System 2 thinking refers to slow thinking where we deliberate. Daniel Kahneman[18] stresses the importance of *effortful reasoning* to resolve moral dilemmas. He maintains that there are times when people need to be engaged in slow deliberate thinking to resolve complex moral dilemmas. Fast or intuitive thinking may lead to a decision which does not address the complexity of a moral dilemma.

Chapter 4: Principled Thinking Model presents a conceptual framework to organize the basic categories and concepts needed to resolve moral dilemmas in pursuit of justice.

Chapters 5-9 present the five categories of the Principled Thinking model (duty, rights, motive, desert, and justice). Numerous examples are used to illustrate how the categories and concepts are used. Each of the five categories of the model (duties, rights, motive, desert, and justice) is presented in several ways. First, the key words and ideas of a category are explained. Second, an alternative subjective view for resolving moral dilemmas is presented based on *Road to Character*[19] by David Brooks. Third, the categories and concepts are presented in hypothetical conversations between two teachers, Mae and Bill, to show how the model might be used in regular conversation.

Part II: Resolving moral dilemmas in pursuit of justice requires a sense of empathy or fellow feeling,

Chapter 10: Cognition and Affect points out that the Principled Thinking Model, which is focused on thinking through moral dilemmas, fails to consider the emotional aspect of moral dilemmas. I draw attention to the advances made about how people think in the late twentieth and early twenty first century in neuroscience. It is acknowledged that neuroscientists raise serious questions about the degree to which people consciously make decisions, including moral decisions. Antonio

Damasio[20] identified the crucial role emotions play in structuring human thought.

Chapter 11: Moral Values Principle Tests developed by Kurt Baier in *The Moral Point of View*[21] introduces the following tests: the New Cases Test, Role Exchange Test, Subsumption Test, and Universal Consequences Test. They challenge people to experience a sense of fellow-feeling or empathy in resolving moral dilemmas. Once again, I acknowledge that even the application of the tests does not necessarily resolve issues (that is, guarantee right answers) but can help to resolve issues of right and wrong.

Chapter 12: Dissonance identifies the kinds of conflict people experience when they encounter moral dilemmas. They can experience, different kinds of dissonance - logical, cultural, experiential, and moral. When people experience dissonance, they try to resolve or reduce it. As we will see, sometimes dissonance may actually interfere with resolving moral dilemmas. Leon Festinger[22] maintains that the most promising form of dissonance for resolving moral dilemmas is cognitive dissonance.

Part III: Application of the Principled Thinking Model and the Moral Values Principle Tests

Moral dilemmas reflect real life problems which seldom arise in neat and organized packages. Nine dilemmas are analyzed to show how critical thinking and a sense of empathy are or are not applied. The conversations between Mae and Bill, which I call *thought experiments*, illustrate how different combinations of the categories and concepts are used to discuss difficult moral dilemmas. They discuss the following issues.

Chapter 13: Censoring Internet Access
Chapter 14: Irate Parent
Chapter 15: Considerate parent
Chapter 16: Arthur's Moral Dilemma
Chapter 17: Cyber Bullying
Chapter 18: Civil Society
Chapter 19: International Responsibilities
Chapter 20: The Enemy Is Neglect of Mental Illness
Chapter 21: Reconciliation

Part IV: What If ...

My goal for this book is to challenge us to use the categories and concepts of the Principled Thinking Model to resolve moral dilemmas in pursuit of justice or fairness. I close with a hypothetical scenario where, in the absence of a sense of fellow-feeling or empathy, principled thinking is not used in resolving a moral dilemma. To that end, I say in the words of David Brooks, "I'm hoping that you and I will both emerge ... slightly different and slightly better."[23]

Part I
Thinking through moral dilemmas in pursuit of justice or fairness

Chapter 1 presents scenarios which point to the need for resolving moral dilemmas in every-day life situations. Two very different situations are presented: a study where young people were interviewed about their approach to resolving moral dilemmas and the emerging application of artificial intelligence to cars. This is followed in Chapter 2 by an introduction to convincing research on how people develop cognition especially as it relates to reasoning used to resolve moral dilemmas. This Chapter is focused on the seminal work of Jean Piaget and Lawrence Kohlberg. In chapter 3, attention is drawn to Daniel Kahnemen's point that effortful reasoning is needed to address some moral dilemmas. Finally in Chapter 4, I introduce the five categories - duty, rights, motive, desert, justice – of the Principled Thinking Model which serves as the core of the book. It is followed by Chapters 5-9 where each of the five categories of the Principled Thinking Model are developed and explained in several different ways.

Chapter 1
Challenge

So you think you can think? Not so fast with your response ... read what David Brooks, columnist for the *New York Times*[24], reported in 2011 on how young people answered questions about *right* and *wrong*. He based the article on a study conducted in 2008 by the Notre Dame sociologist Christian Smith that involved in-depth interviews with 230 young adults from across America. Smith's research team asked the young adults open-ended questions about right and wrong, moral dilemmas and the meaning of life.

Brooks reported that ... "when asked to describe a moral dilemma they had faced, two-thirds of the young people either couldn't answer the question or [shifted to describe] problems that were not moral at all."[25]

When asked about wrong or evil, the respondents generally agreed that rape and murder qualified as such. But, aside from agreeing on these two issues, moral thinking (e.g., thinking about right and wrong) didn't enter the picture for them, even when they considered issues like drunk driving, cheating in school or cheating on a partner.

The default position, that most of them came back to again and again, was that moral choices are just a matter of personal viewpoints. "It's personal," the respondents typically said. "It's up to the individual. Who am I to say?"[26]

Brooks concluded that "they [the young people] just don't have the categories or concepts to answer questions about right and wrong[27] This inability to think about moral issues can have major implications, because moral issues are part of daily life.

I agree with Brooks. Take for example the futuristic concept of driver-less cars. Besides the positive benefit of reducing the carbon footprint, the use of driverless cars raises several issues. Consider the causal, legal and moral issues raised by the following excerpt from an incident report in The Canadian Press by Justin Pritchard in 2016:

> On Valentine's Day a Google vehicle struck the side of a public bus in the Silicon Valley city of Mountain View. Footage recorded by cameras shows a Lexus SUV, which Google had outfitted with sensors and cameras to enable it to drive itself, edging into the path of the bus that was rolling by at about 15 mph.
>
> The transit agency concluded that the bus driver was not responsible, spokeswoman Stacey Hendler Ross said. An independent claims adjustor has not yet determined liability.
>
> Google has said that both the car's software and the person in the driver's seat thought the bus would let the Lexus into the flow of traffic.
>
> This is a classic example of the negotiation that's a normal part of driving -- we're all trying to predict each other's movements."In this case, we clearly bear some responsibility because, if our car hadn't moved, there wouldn't have been a collision," Google wrote of the incident.[28]

The Transit Agency and Department of Motor Vehicles have the responsibility of resolving the questions of what caused the accident, and the courts have the responsibility of settling the legal responsibilities of the companies which produced the car or the software developer. The real challenge was resolving the moral issues regarding the decision to edge into the path of an oncoming bus. This raises the question: "How can artificial intelligence (AI) make the decisions about right and wrong actions?" Traditionally, human drivers make these decisions, but in this case they were made by the (AI) of the self-driving car.

On June 30, 2016, *The Washington Post* reported the first fatality involving a self-driving car:

A Tesla driver was killed in a collision in Florida with a tractor trailer while the vehicle was in Autopilot mode. Tesla reported that "It is the first known fatality in more than 130 million miles driven with autopilot activated." .... The Washington Post reported that "Bryan Thomas, a spokesman for the National Highway Traffic Safety Administration, said it was investigating the fatality to see if the autopilot system was to blame." Tesla acknowledged that the accident might have been the fault of the computer.[29]

This fatality heightens the challenge of resolving the moral issues related to self-driving cars. At best, the AI in a car can be programmed to make decisions about consequences. For example, if the car veered into oncoming traffic due to mechanical failure, AI could be programmed to identify the failure. But that is not what moral judgments are all about. The driver-less car also had to address issues of right and wrong, namely, the decision to put people in the car and the bus at risk of injury or death by edging the car into the path of the bus. Can AI make right and wrong decisions in pursuit of justice? What concepts and thinking are required to make these moral decisions? To address this question, requires an understanding of how people of all ages develop the ability to think through moral issues. Cognitive development psychology addresses this question. Since this book is focused on resolving moral dilemmas, we need to know more about the development of moral reasoning.

Chapter 2
Cognitive development

Cognitive development, according to Jonathan Haidt[30], is focused on how people think and develop. Piaget illustrates this development by focusing on the thinking errors children make. For example, he poured water into two identical glasses and asked pre-school children which glass held the most water. Unanimously, they said that both glasses held the same amount of water. Then he poured the content of one of the glasses into a tall skinny glass and asked the children to compare the tall glass of water with the other glass. Unanimously, they said the tall glass contains more water. They did not understand that the total volume of water in the tall glass had not changed. Prompting children to help them understand the correct answer was pointless. They will not understand till they reach the age (and cognitive stage) where their minds are ready to understand the concept of conservation. They have to figure it out for themselves. Another example is the Muller-Lyer illusion in Figure 1 where pre-school children are asked to identify which strait line is longer. They thought the top line was longer because it looked longer.

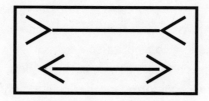

Figure 1: Muller-Lyer illusion

The research in cognitive development psychology by clinical psychologist, Jean Piaget[31], and psychologist, Lawrence Kohlberg[32], suggests people can acquire the categories and concepts necessary to engage in moral thinking. By paying careful attention to what children say, Piaget concluded that children pass through stages of moral thinking about obligations and rights. Over time, they can develop an understanding of increasingly complex reciprocal forms of thought. Piaget identified four levels or stages of thought: Sensory motor stage, pre-operational or representational stage, concrete operational stage, and formal hypothetical deductive reasoning stage. During the first two years after birth, children develop practical intelligence; they are pre-occupied with action and not ideas. Their dominant form of thought from ages two to seven is intuition. At this stage of development, children form representational images of what they perceive through their senses. The emergence of the ability to form logical operations occurs from seven to twelve. At this stage, children display an understanding of "smaller than" and "larger than" (adding and subtracting). Piaget calls this concrete operational thought. During early adolescence, children usually become capable of hypothetical-deductive reasoning. They discover principles which they apply in various situations. They are intrigued by possible solutions to problems.

Piaget applied this cognitive developmental approach to the study of children's moral thinking. He maintained that children's understanding of morality is similar to their understanding of conservation as in the two glasses activity described above. Piaget went on to identify two basic categories of understanding: heteronomy (absolute respect for authority) and autonomy (freedom from external control), which are reflected, for example, in people's concept of cooperation. Children's concept of cooperation is characterized by unilateral respect (one way respect) whereas adult's concept of cooperation generally is characterized by mutual respect (two way respect). In short, what is most significant in Piaget's observation about the development of moral thinking is that the same moral concept can mean different things to different people depending on their level of development. This difference seems to reflect different ways of understanding obligations and rights which are two of the five key categories for moral thinking in the Principled Thinking Model developed in Part I of this book.

Lawrence Kohlberg followed up on Piaget's work by identifying an invariant sequence of stages of moral development reflecting Piaget's stages of moral thinking. Through cross-cultural and longitudinal studies, Kohlberg identified the following six stages[33]

Stages of Moral Development

Pre-conventional level
      Stage 1 - Punishment and obedience orientation
      Stage 2 - Instrumental relativist orientation
Conventional level
      Stage 3 - interpersonal concordance orientation
      Stage 4 - law and order orientation
Pre-conventional level
      Stage 5 - Social contract orientation
      Stage 6 - Universal ethical-principle orientation

Figure 2: Kohlberg's stages of moral development

At the Pre-conventional level, a child operates on the basis of what's considered good and bad, right and wrong as defined by his cultural environment. The child identifies them by the punishment or reward consequences of his action. Kohlberg identified two stages.

Stage 1 is strictly a matter of avoiding punishment. Power is considered right; therefore everyone must be obedient. No sense of moral values is displayed in that no distinction is drawn between moral worth of human life and physical or social values. For example, when a child under the age of seven breaks a glass, he expects to be punished immediately. Nor does he make a difference between breaking a glass and striking his sister. Both actions are wrong and he deserves to be punished for both.

At stage 2, the main concern is for the satisfaction of one's own needs and sometimes the needs of significant others. The value of human life is a matter of the way it satisfies one's own needs and sometimes the needs of others. For example, when Tommy and Billy sorted pennies, Tommy collected more pennies than Billy. When Grandma asked him to share some of his pennies with Billy, he refused. However, if there had been something in it for Tommy to share some of his pennies with Billy, he might have agreed to share some. If Grandma had offered to give both boys two candies each, Tommy might have agreed to share provided that it is the only way he could get the candies.

At the Conventional level, a person displays a concern for group loyalty. The expectations of the group take precedence over one's immediate consequences. Kohlberg identified two stages.

At stage 3, good behavior is that which pleases or helps others and is approved by them. Behavior is frequently judged by intentions or motives. For example, the affective relationship among families is considered important. Had Tommy been a little older, age twelve and up, he might have agreed to share some of his pennies with Billy in order to please his Grandma. After all, he loves his Grandma.

At stage 4, there is an awareness of social order and a concern to maintain it through rules and doing one's duty. The value of life is determined by a universal order of rights and duties which nobody has a right to tamper with. Had Tommy and Billy been teenagers, Tommy might have agreed to share some of his pennies with Billy, because Tommy might have understood that it was his duty to do what Grandma asked him to do. He might have also recognized that Billy probably had a right to an equal number of pennies.

At the Post-conventional level, autonomous or principled moral judgments are made independently of authority and the individual's immediate interest. Again, Kohlberg identified two stages.

At stage 5, the social contract legalistic orientation is modified by taking into account social utility. There is a clear awareness of the relativism of personal values and procedural rules for reaching a consensus. Life is valued, both, in terms of the welfare of the community and of being a universal human right. Suppose as young adults, Bill and Tom decided to form a company to develop websites for other companies. Their lawyer prepared a shareholder's agreement for them to make them equal partners. Suppose the company failed after it accrued considerable debt. Since they had agreed to be equal partners, they both paid an equal portion of the debt because they treasured their relationship as brothers and respected their mutual rights and responsibilities.

At stage 6, the universal ethical-principle orientation reflects a truly autonomous person who acts on the basis of self-chosen ethical principles grounded in logical consistency and universality. The principles are abstract (e.g., the Golden Rule) and not concrete (e.g., The Ten Commandments). People at this stage express a belief in the sacredness of human life as representing a universal human value of respect for the individual. As mature adults running a successful consulting business, Tom and Bill would have viewed life differently again. When their neighbour, suffered a major loss due to a fire at his factory, Tom and Bill might have offered free consulting services to their neighbour to refinance his business to restore his plant. Why? They followed the Golden Rule even though they were not obligated to help their neighbour. They wanted to help their neighbour to have a second opportunity to provide for his family and serve his community. Imagine what the world would look like if everyone followed the Golden Rule.

In addition to focusing on rights and responsibilities, Kohlberg's stages reflect specific motives for moral action at each stage. At stage 1, children are motivated by the avoidance of punishment – reflecting an irrational fear of punishment. At stage two, children are motivated by a desire for a reward or benefit. At stage three, children are motivated by the approval by others. At stage four, adolescents are motivated by group censure or failure of doing one's duty. At stage five, people are motivated by respect for equality and community. At stage six, people are motivated by a concern about self-condemnation for violating one's own principles.

Kohlberg refers to the process of transitioning from one stage to the next as 'assimilating and accommodating' to achieve equilibrium. Leon

Festinger, in *A Theory of Cognitive Dissonance*[34] describes it as a constant process of dissonance generation and reduction to achieve equilibrium. As I explain in Chapter 12, equilibrium is not assured because the dissonance can take on several forms – logical, cultural, experiential or cognitive. Kohlberg maintains that only the later can result in cognitive development.

Kohlberg offers a psychological basis for claiming that stage six is the highest level of moral development. Again, he appeals to the criteria of differentiation and integration through the process of dissonance generation and reduction. He illustrates this through an analysis of how the universal moral categories, *rights* and *duty*, are expressed differently at each stage of development[35.] Kohlberg claims that *rights* and *duties* are universal in that all cultures he reviewed acknowledged them. Let me illustrate the development of a sense of *rights* and *duty* by comparing stage one to stage six:

> *Stage 1: Punishment and obedience orientation*
>
> At this stage, *having a right* means having the power or authority to control something or someone. A child under the age of seven expects to be punished by someone in authority for breaking a glass or striking his sister. Both actions are wrong and the child deserves to be punished by an authority. The child's parent or teacher has a right to punish him.
>
> Obligation: or *should* refers to what one *has to do* because of the demands of external authorities, rules or situations. A child expects authorities (e.g., parents) to punish him because they have authority over him[35].
>
> There is no correlativity between individual rights and duties at stage one. A person accepts whatever *rights* another person ascribes to him or her. For example, a child accepts whatever *rights* an adult says she has even

if the adult does not have authority to determine the child's *rights*.

Stage 6: Universal ethical-principle orientation

At this stage, *having a right* refers to the universal right of *just* treatment which goes beyond liberties. It represents a universal claim of one individual upon another.

As I mentioned before, as mature adults running a successful financial consulting business, Tom and Bill would view life differently. When their neighbour, suffered a major loss due to a fire at his factory, Tom and Bill offered free financial consulting services to help their neighbour restore his plant. They felt their neighbour had a *right* to expect as much from his neighbour.

Obligation: refers to *having a right* or *just* claim by an individual to a corresponding *duty* to another individual. Following the Golden Rule, Tom and Bill felt obligated to help their neighbour to have a second opportunity to provide for his family and serve his community[36].

The use of the concept *rights* and *duties* illustrate how the higher stage (stage 6) is more differentiated and integrated than prior stages. At stage 6, *rights* and *duties* are totally correlative; they belong together. The correlative to *rights* is present in the statement, "for every *right* people have, society has a *duty* to protect that *right*."

Reversibility is another concept central to Kohlberg's sense of moral thought. To say that *rights* and *duties* are correlative is to say that one can move back and forth between them without distortion. In other words, *fairness* is attained through reversibility in the sense that a moral decision requires that all interested parties agree to consider their own claims impartially. Each person in the agreement arrives at the same decision as he/she puts him or herself in the shoes of the other. Reversibility implies universality and reciprocity. For example, take the incident in the Preface involving Jack and Peter where the principal asked the boys, "What's the right thing to do going forward?" Jack did not consider his response from the perspective of putting himself in Peter's shoes. Would Jack have insisted on the same form of punishment if he had been in Peter's place? That's doubtful; he would not have considered it fair to lose a whole school year over one fight if that punishment were applied to himself.

Kohlberg identified *justice* as the universal fundamental principle. He claims that by stage six, *authority* and *utility* are replaced by the universal principle of *justice* as a way of resolving conflicting actions.

Studies to date suggest a moderate degree of correlation between moral judgment and behavior. Types of behavior that have been studied include cheating on a quiz, confessing to a misdeed and touching a forbidden toy[37].

I acknowledge that there are a number of difficulties with Kohlberg's philosophical assertions. However, I draw attention to one issue in particular: Is morality strictly a cognitive exercise as suggested by Kohlberg's cognitive development approach? Is there no role for the affect? One of the central arguments made by the critics of Kohlberg's view of development is that people make moral judgments not only from a cognitive perspective when they are confronted with moral issues. Here is what the critics have to say.

Jeremy Rifkin[38], senior lecturer at the Wharton School's Executive Education Program at the University of Pennsylvania, takes issue with Kohlberg's focus on cognition. Rifkin maintains that Kohlberg reflects the famous statement by Descartes in the seventeen century, "I think, therefore I am". Rifkin maintains that "it's the very feelings and emotions they [rationalists] discount that allow human beings to develop empathic bonds." He goes on to say "Without feelings and emotions, empathy does not exist. A world without empathy is alien to the very notion of what a human being is[39]." In contrast to Kohlberg's view, Rifkin describes his view as "I participate, therefore I am[40]."

I pay so much attention to cognitive development because it is a fundamental part of the development experienced by people along with physical, social, emotional and sexual development. Kohlberg presents the development of increasingly differentiated and integrated conception of *duties, rights, motive,* and *justice.* People need moral language to increasingly differentiated and integrated levels of thinking.

Chapter 3
Effortful Reasoning

In *Thinking Fast and Slow*, Daniel Kahneman[41], Professor of Psychology at Princeton University and recipient of the 2002 Nobel Prize in Economic Science, stressed the importance of moral reasoning with his description of System 1 and System 2 thinking. System 1 thinking refers to fast or intuitive thinking which depends on trial and error practices, perception (see, hear, or become aware of), and memory (instant recall). It refers to the instant responses we make in spontaneous situations. System 2 thinking refers to slow thinking where we deliberate, which he describes as an effortful form of thinking, a more engaged and analytic mode. This raises the following question, "Are there situations where people tend to resolve dilemmas through fast intuitive thinking when, in fact, the situation requires slow deliberate thinking? Are moral dilemmas such situations?" Kahneman says yes. He shares his personal story from his Psychotherapy class to explain what he means:

> You will from time to time meet a patient who shares a disturbing tale of multiple mistakes in his previous treatment. He has been seen by several clinicians, and all failed him. The patient can lucidly describe how his therapists misunderstood him, but he has quickly perceived that you are different. You share the same feeling, are convinced that you understand him, and will be able to help[42].

Kahneman observed the students' feeling of sympathy towards the patient, and his firm advice to the students was, "Do not even think of taking on this patient. He is most likely a psychopath and you will not be able to help him." Kahneman points out that the System 1 feeling of sympathy was the students' instantaneous response and it was wrong. The students had not exercised System 2 deliberations. In short, he alerts us to the risk of using System 1 thinking in situations where System 2 thinking is needed. The Principled Thinking Model presented in this book outlines categories and concepts for System 2 thinking.

In the case of the young people in the Study reviewed by Brooks, it could be argued that their response to questions of right and wrong, namely, "It's up to the individual. Who am I to say?" is an example of System 1 fast thinking. Take for example, the issue of cheating on an exam in school which the young people did not consider to be a moral issue based on their fast or intuitive thinking. Suppose they would have taken the time to think about the implications of some students cheating on an exam and others not. Suppose one of the cheaters received a scholarship because he out-performed students who did not cheat. Would that be fair? What if the non-cheating student was your sister; would that make any difference to your views on cheating? Thinking through this scenario and related questions might have generated a different response from the young people. The two different responses illustrate the distinction between system 1 and System 2 thinking.

In the Steubenville case, Richard Cohen offers the following summary in *Miley Cyrus, Steubenville and teen culture run amok*:

> ... what indisputably did happen is troubling enough. A teenage girl, stone-drunk, was stripped and manhandled. She was photographed and the picture passed around. Obviously, she was sexually mistreated. And while many people knew about all of this, no one did anything about it. The girl was dehumanized ... As Levy (a New York writer) put it, "The teens seemed largely unaware that they'd been involved in a crime." She quoted the Jefferson County prosecutor, Jane Hanlin, who said,

"They don't think that what they've seen is a rape in the classic sense[43].

At the same time, Cohen's view of most teenagers is encouraging provided they are asked to reflect on a different but related question when they have time to think about it:

> ... if you were to interview a thousand teen-agers before this case happened and asked this question, "Is it illegal to take a video of another teenager naked?" I would be astonished if you could find even one who said yes[44].

Cohen suggested that teenagers are quite capable of knowing right from wrong when they have time to think about it. That's why he thinks the young people would have responded very differently to the question: "Is it illegal to take a video of another teenager naked[45]?" They would have insisted that it is illegal and wrong. Their response to the later question would have been a System 2 response.

Antonio Damagio, David Dornsife Professor of Neuroscience, Psychology and Neurology, and director of Brain and Creativity Institute at the Southern California University, in the book *Self Comes to Mind* reinforces the importance of Kahneman's slow thinking by pointed out that " unconscious forces are influenced by the on-going process of conceptualizing, testing and reasoning that takes place in the conscious mind[46]." In other words, the "unconscious forces" of System 1 fast thinking can and need to be influenced by System 2 effortful reasoning in difficult situations. The Principled Thinking Model offers categories and concepts for the process described by Damagio.

Chapter 4
Principled Thinking Model

So, what are the categories of the Principled Thinking Model (PTM) which, as I stated in the Introduction, serve as a foundation for our every day efforts to be fair and just in our relationships at home, at work and in society at large? The fundamental categories of the model are: rights, duties, motive, desert and justice or fairness (Figure 3). How can we use them to arrive at just and fair decisions?

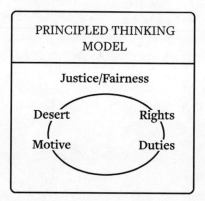

Figure 3: Categories of the Principled Thinking Model

Remember the story about Jack and Peter. Jack insisted that Peter deserved a very serious form of punishment: expulsion from school for the rest of the school year. Jack did not assume any responsibility for the fight with Peter. The principal had the responsibility of helping the boys resolve their problem in a fair way which would require thinking about assuming responsibility for one's action, determining what people deserve, being fair, just to mention a few issues.

Each category of the Principled Thinking Model is explained in detail in several ways in the following chapters. First, the main concepts of a category are identified and illustrated. For example the concept, wrong, under the category "duty" is used in the moral sense in the sentence: "It is wrong for children to pick on the new classmate." The term is used in a non-moral or epistemic sense in the sentence: "He gave the wrong answer to that math question."

Second, a contrasting subjective view held by some young people as presented in the study by Christian Smith and in the book, *The Road to Character*, by Brooks is presented. For example, the young people in the study believe that "assuming responsibility" means, "Your personal feelings are the best guide for what is right and wrong[47]."

Third, thought experiments are used to show how these concepts might be applied in ordinary moral discourse. This is done through hypothetical conversations involving the categories and concepts of PTM by two teachers, Mae and Bill who teach 9th graders at Middletown Middle School. Both are quite eager to push an argument as far as they can. Here is one example.

> Mae raised a new question, "If an act is morally right, is it a person's duty to do it?"

> "Not necessarily," Bill replied. "Just because it may be morally right for you to offer to cover my recess duty, does not mean that it is your duty to do it."

In the following chapters, each category includes a number of concepts. Figure 4 identifies some of the key concepts for each of the five categories of the Principled Thinking Model. As I have explained above, the concepts for each category are explained and illustrated.

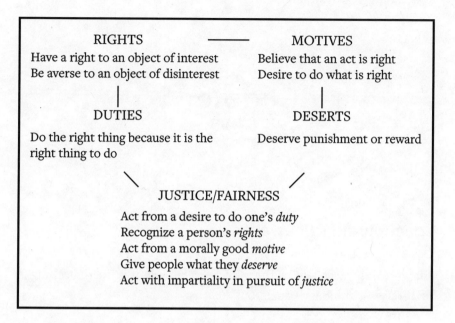

RIGHTS ——— MOTIVES
Have a right to an object of interest   Believe that an act is right
Be averse to an object of disinterest   Desire to do what is right

DUTIES   DESERTS
Do the right thing because it is the   Deserve punishment or reward
right thing to do

JUSTICE/FAIRNESS
Act from a desire to do one's *duty*
Recognize a person's *rights*
Act from a morally good *motive*
Give people what they *deserve*
Act with impartiality in pursuit of *justice*

Figure 4: Key concepts of the Principled Thinking Model

Chapter 5
Duty

Conceptual Framework

The word *duty* means doing the right thing because it is the right thing to do. It raises a number of questions such as:

- Are there degrees of rightness?
- Are there degrees of wrongness?
- Does ought imply can?
- Are people's acts determined or do people act from free will?
- Are judgments about beliefs, attitudes, feeling, emotions and thoughts moral judgments?

Duty also includes the following words which, I am certain, you have used many times:

> obligation, right, wrong, responsible, forbidden, ought, prescribe, should, permissible, must, may, bound, correct, sinful, moral, immoral, ethical, unethical[48]

Some of the nouns we commonly use in moral discourse referring to wrong acts include: crime, moral transgression, and moral offence. Crime refers to acts which are more serious than offences.

Key words

Duty is used, in this book, in the moral sense unless otherwise indicated. Some of the terms related to duty can also be used in a non-moral sense. For example, the term, *wrong*, is used in the moral sense in the sentence: It is wrong for children to pick on the new child in class. The term is used in a non-moral or epistemic sense in the sentence: He gave the wrong answer to that math question. Other examples of using terms in the moral sense include: *responsible* means morally responsible, *incumbent* means morally incumbent, *permissible* means morally permissible.

Sometimes people engage in acts which are done *beyond the call of duty*. They are called acts of supererogation. That many people consider such acts as right acts is evident from the fact that the military bestows honors, like the Victoria Cross, on people who perform heroic acts by going beyond the call of duty.

We know that sometimes doing one's duty is not an object of interest but an *object of disinterest*. It may be one's duty to pay taxes even though this is regarded as an object of disinterest, something many taxpayers would rather not do. On the other hand, it may be a coach's duty to coach a basketball team at his school and it may also be an object of interest for that coach.

Did you ever notice that *obligation* and *duty* tend to have the same definition but are used in different ways? A person can put someone under an obligation but not under a duty (e.g., having an obligation to keep your promise). Obligations tend to be incurred as the result of something a person has done. The obligation *to keep ones promise* follows from the fact that a person made a promise to keep his promise. On the other hand, a person has a *duty* in virtue of his situation and the person he is. If Mr. Smith is a qualified teacher hired by a school board, then he has a duty to teach because he is someone who has been hired by a school board to be a teacher and because he is a qualified teacher. If he was not a qualified teacher, however *qualified* is defined, he would not have an actual duty to teach.

A *responsibility* is a duty which a person has by virtue of her particular position. Often, we feel a sense of responsibility whenever we have assumed a new position or career. A parent has a responsibility to provide her child with proper nutrition by virtue of the fact that she is the child's parent. A teacher has a responsibility to teach her students by virtue of the fact that she is their teacher.

Some terms have acquired a rather specialized meaning. For example, the term *immoral* as used today frequently seems to refer to sexual morality. This seems to be the meaning of, "You cannot legislate morality" which means that the sexual life of citizens cannot be governed or controlled through legislation.

Observe the *normative* and *descriptive* use of the antonyms of *moral*. When *moral* is used in the normative sense, its antonym is *immoral*, but when it is used in the descriptive sense, its antonym is *non-moral*.

Morally forbidden simply means it is morally wrong to do an action.

Notice the flexible usage of the term *morally permissible*. To say that an act is morally permissible means that it is not wrong to do it. It could be a right or a morally indifferent act. For example, the statement, "It is morally permissible for you to lend your bicycle to your neighbour" means that it is not morally wrong. It could be the right thing to do or it could be a morally indifferent act. On the other hand, it would be morally wrong to lend your neighbour's bicycle to someone else without permission from your neighbour.

The meaning of the term *may do* is even more flexible. To say that a person may do a certain act is to say that it is not wrong to do the act. For example, "You may walk or ride your bicycle to school" means you are free to choose between the two options.

Right and wrong are not *contradictory* terms but *contrary* terms. Contrary refers to terms that are opposites or opposed to each other. Right actions and wrong actions are opposites. On the other hand, contradictory statement cannot both be true; they cannot both be right and wrong. For example, mocking a new immigrant student cannot be both, right and wrong. It is wrong.

Key ideas

I begin with one of the most basic concepts people face every day: *doing one's duty*. If it is a person's duty to do something then the act of doing it is morally right and it would be wrong not to do it. However, the converse, "If an act is morally right, it is a person's duty to do it" does not seem to follow. In other words, *morally right action* does not necessarily mean, "It is a person's duty to do it". Suppose it is right for a teacher to give a student a dollar to buy a lunch. This does not mean that the teacher has a duty to give the student a dollar. It may be right to send the student home to pick up his lunch or for a school to offer a lunch program.

Doing one's duty can refer to several different levels of commitment. First, it can mean that a person simply follow his duty. A person simply follows whatever duty has been assigned to him. If James needs to finish editing his high school history essay which is due the next day, he will not join his friends for a birthday party because he needs to submit his essay on time. Second, it can mean wanting to do one's duty. The person shows intent: *wanting to do one's duty*. This intent reflects a stronger commitment. James may also want to submit his essay on time because he wants to compete for a scholarship. He cannot afford to lose a point or two for submitting an assignment late. Third, it can mean *wanting to do one's duty because it is the right thing to do*. A person identifies a condition for doing one's duty, *wanting to do what is right*. James may want to submit his paper on time because he wants to do the right thing for his history teacher who has to read all the papers from his class, reflect on them and score them. Late papers might make it more difficult for the teacher to get his work done in a timely manner.

It is important to be aware of certain issues that arise in the use of the terms right and wrong in moral discourse. For example, *Are there degrees of rightness as well as degrees of wrongness?* The answer to the first part of this question is simple; there are no degrees of rightness. An act is either right or not. For example, "Children should be fair to each other" cannot be half right or partially right or very right. It is simply the right thing to do.

On the other hand, there are degrees of wrongness. One act can be more seriously wrong than another. For example, it is considered by most people more seriously wrong to injure a person than to injure a dog. Both are considered wrong but not to the same degree. This distinction is reflected in ordinary moral conversation as well as in the fact that a person would be punished more severely for injuring a person than a dog.

Another issue regarding the use of the terms right and wrong is: *Does it follow from the fact that an act is right that not doing it is wrong?* The answer to this question is more complicated. It may be wrong not to do the act and it need not be wrong. If it is a person's duty to support the inter-scholastic sports programs, then it is right to support it and wrong not to support it. On the other hand, it may be right for a parent to volunteer as an assistant coach in her child's school but it would not be wrong not to volunteer as a coach.

A critic might be tempted to ask, *Are there no morally indifferent acts?* To argue that there are no morally indifferent acts seems contrary to common sense. Some acts are neither right nor wrong; they are morally indifferent. For example, watching the World Series on TV is neither, right or wrong; it is a morally indifferent act.

However, the statement, *It is not a question of whether this action is right* leaves open the possibility that the action might be morally indifferent. *I don't think that's wrong* may refer to an act as being morally indifferent. For example, to say, "I don't think it is wrong for children to play soccer after school" is not saying that it is right or wrong to play soccer after school; it may simply be a morally indifferent act.

A third issue concerning the use of the terms right and wrong is about the *person making the decision* about an act being right or wrong. The person making the judgment must meet three conditions: a) distinguish between right and wrong, b) have a concept of right and wrong and c) understand the meaning of right and wrong. A non-moral person does not meet these conditions and therefore cannot judge the morality of an act.

It has been suggested by some that a moral person has to *be able to speak*, but, that is doubtful. The ability to speak may help others know whether a person is a moral person. However, a person may show the difference between right and wrong through her actions. Helen Keller (1880 - 1968), an American author, was the first deaf/blind person to graduate from college. She campaigned for women's suffrage and labour rights. Ludwig Van Beethoven (1770-1827) was able to create music and play music even after being completely deaf. He composed his final and greatest symphony, Beethoven's Ninth Symphony, when he was completely deaf.

Who or what is a non-moral being? Animals are generally considered to be non-moral beings. A person may be a non-moral person if he suffers from psychosocial pathologies to the extent that he cannot have a sense of right and wrong. Although it is recognized that children are not capable of making certain moral judgments, they are considered moral persons because, as they develop, they become increasingly more capable of making moral judgments. In short, *non-moral being* does not refer only to animals but can also refer to people.

You might ask, *What about a-moral people?* He or she is someone who does not have a concept of right and wrong but is potentially capable of making moral judgments. It could be someone who was brought up in total isolation. It includes sociopaths who suffer from an antisocial personality disorder which includes a total disregard for and violation of the rights of others.

Another issue to keep in mind about duty is the famous assertion: *Ought implies can*. A person must be capable of what is morally expected of him. Without it, *ought* simply does not apply. A person cannot be responsible for his actions unless he is in his right mind and capable of assuming responsibility for his action.

What if a person is not in his right mind because of some action he took, such as consuming too much alcohol? Suppose Paul gets involved in a brawl at school as a result of consuming too much alcohol? Was his action (i.e., getting involved in a brawl) wrong due to his consumption of too much alcohol or due to his getting involved in a brawl? Would it not have been wrong for him to have consumed too much alcohol if he had not gotten involved in a brawl?

Paul's action is wrong on both counts: wrong due to his consumption of too much alcohol and due to getting involved in a brawl. Why? By consuming too much alcohol, he put himself out of a state of being in his right mind. He put himself into a situation where he could not do what he ought to do. Since he acted under the influence of alcohol which impaired his ability to make a moral judgment, his responsibility was diminished to some degree.

What if a person committed a wrong act in a fit of anger? Whether the person committed a morally wrong act would depend on whether he had any control or influence over his circumstances. If the fit of anger was brought on by failing grades due to lack of effort, he could have influenced his circumstances and therefore he would be responsible for his fit of anger. If, on the other hand, the fit of anger was brought on by a malfunctioning of his brain such as brain tumors, aneurysms, head trauma or blocked blood vessels that can burst and trigger a stroke, he would not be responsible The person would have lost control due to his special circumstances and therefore he should not be held responsible for his action.

Are members of youth gangs who cause injury and destruction, moral persons? They could be. A person can have the concepts of right and wrong but need not be influenced by them. Such a person is considered to be unscrupulous.

The concepts of *freedom of will and determinism* affect our understanding of morality. First, I state the obvious. Not only must a person be a moral person and be in his right mind so that he is capable of assuming responsibility for his action, he must also be free to make moral judgments. Without this freedom he could not be responsible for what he does.

However the complexity of this issue lingers. Determinism means events have causes. *Freedom of will* refers to the belief that human beings can determine their own actions. People who accept this view reject the idea that human actions are determined by external conditions. Are *freedom of will* and *determinism* really all that different from each other? The difficulty of this question becomes apparent in the question: Is the act of choosing determined or does it have a cause? Suppose Sally, who appreciates classical instrumental music, decides to attend the opening concerts of the local symphony. Was she driven by some involuntary biochemical algorithm in her brain to make this decision as Yuval Harari[30] speculates? But, if choosing is not caused, it would be like a bolt out of the blue. If that were so, how could a person be held responsible for what he chose? If choices are not caused by something, they would be inexplicable. It might seem then that freedom of will need not exclude determinism.

Freedom of will seems to refer to choices determined by reasons rather than by causes. But, reasons may be just another set of causes. Even if the distinction between causes and reasons was established, it is not certain that the problem of freedom of will vs. determinism would be solved. This seems to be an intractable problem. People generally assume that they can make moral judgments. In other words, they assume that people actually can make judgments of right and wrong suggesting that people have, to some degree, freedom of will to make moral decisions.

Finally, there are two more issues related to the conditions for an act to be right or wrong. First, *"Can a person have a conflict of duties?"* As I explain in a scenario later, a person can have a *prima facie* conflict of duties but not an actual conflict of duties. A *prima facie* conflict of duties is a conflict at first glance or an apparent conflict. However, since a person cannot perform both conflicting duties at the same time, he does not have an actual conflict of duties.

The second issue is: *What may be proper objects of right and wrong judgments?* In other words, what sorts of things should be judged to be right or wrong? For example, should beliefs, attitudes, feelings, and emotions be judged to be right or wrong? Since they are mental states, they should not be judged to be right or wrong. A person cannot cease to have a particular mental state such as a particular feeling or emotion by choosing not to have it. Similarly, a person cannot arbitrarily cease to have a certain attitude although a person can cultivate certain attitudes. It could be wrong for a person to fail to cultivate certain attitudes. It would be wrong for a person to fail to cultivate an attitude of not being prejudiced against certain races. The same applies to thinking certain thoughts and have certain beliefs. A person cannot prevent a certain thought from crossing his mind. Since some beliefs are couched in a person's cultural background, they are inherited. However, it would be wrong for a person not to cultivate the practice of carefully reviewing his thoughts. In short, it is problematic to judge thoughts, beliefs, attitudes, feelings, and emotions as being morally right or wrong.

Figure 5 provides a summary of the concepts in the class, duty.

Assumptions about Duty
1. Duty means doing the right thing because it is the right thing to do.
2. A duty is the right thing to do independently of a person's motive or interest.
3. An action is morally right or wrong independently of a person's likes or dislikes.
4. One can put someone under an obligation but not under a duty.
5. If it is a person's duty to do something, then the act of doing it is morally right and it would be wrong not to do it.
6. A person is not necessarily obligated to do every morally right act.

7. Going beyond the call of duty is called an act of supererogation.

8. Doing one's duty may or may not be an object of interest.

9. Immoral must be distinguished from non-moral and a-moral.

10. Nouns referring to immoral acts include: crime, moral transaction, offence.

11. A morally permissible act is not morally wrong; it could be morally right or morally indifferent.

12. If a person may do an act, it is not wrong to do or not to do it.

13. There are no degrees of rightness.

14. There are degrees of the seriousness of wrong acts.

15. If an act is right than not doing it may or may not be wrong.

16. There are morally indifferent acts.

17. What conditions have to be fulfilled for a person to determine whether an act is right or wrong? A person must distinguish between right and wrong, have a concept of right and wrong, and understand the meaning of right and wrong.

18. A moral person can distinguish between right and wrong, has a concept of right and wrong, and understands the meaning of right and wrong.

19. Ought implies can.

20. It is not clear whether people's acts are determined or whether people act from free will.

21. It is not clear whether choosing is determined or whether it has a cause.

22. A person can have a *prima facia* conflict of duties but not an actual conflict of duties.
23. A duty has to be something a person can do or refrain from doing.
24. Judgments about beliefs, attitudes feeling, emotions and thoughts are not moral judgments.

Figure 5: Duty

Young people's view of duty

Brooks offers the following observations about youth's perceptions of right and wrong.

The young people would concur with the non-moral epistemic meaning. Brooks observes that they "trust the self and distrust the conventions of the outer world[49]." Reference to a normative usage seems irrelevant to them since the issue of right and wrong is a personal matter.

They insist that a person does not have a duty. Brooks quotes Carl Rogers who maintains when a person "can be freely in touch with his valuing process in himself, he will behave in ways that are self-enhancing[50]."

How can a person go beyond the call of duty if right action simply refers to one's personal perception of right and wrong? It's not clear that they can.

For them the distinction between objects of interest and objects of disinterest is purely personal. Again, Brooks, quoting Rogers, says that young people maintain that they are "moving with subtle and ordered complexity towards the goal the organism is endeavoring to achieve[51]".

Whether a person has an obligation to keep ones promise is strictly a matter of personal choice. An obligation *to keep your promise* does not follow from the fact that you have made that promise. Hence, there seems to be no point to making a promise.

We all make choices. Brooks describes their way of making choices this way, "Your personal feelings are the best guide for what is right and wrong[52]." But this brings up the troubling question of how can any action be morally forbidden when right and wrong is simply up to the individual? Brooks further explains that, for them "the valid rules of life are those you make or accept for yourself and that feel right to you[53]." All acts, for the young people Brooks refers to, could potentially be morally permissible.

Brooks describes degrees of right and wrong as perceived by young people this way, "I know I am doing right because I feel harmonious inside. Something is going wrong, on the other hand, when I feel I am not being true to myself[54]." Any and all acts are morally indifferent acts except rape and murder according to them.

No external conditions need to be fulfilled for an action to be right or wrong. Brooks describes their view this way, "One True Self has no basis to judge or argue with another True Self.... you become an individualist, since the ultimate arbiter is the authentic arbiter within and not any community standard or external horizon of significance[55]."

The young people would agree that a person cannot be held responsible for his actions unless he is in his right mind. The problem lies with their use of the term, responsibilities. For them, "Your desires are like inner oracles for what is right and true.[56]."

Ought implies can is irrelevant for people who claim they are not obligated to do anything unless they personally want to do it. The young people maintain that "the self is to be trusted, not doubted[57]."

They would accept that a person should not be held accountable whenever he acts from a fit of anger if it is brought on by a malfunctioning of a gland or by neurons in the brain.

Brooks maintains that the following quote from Charles Taylor applies to the young people, "There is a certain way of being that is my way. I am called to live my life in this way and not in imitation of anyone else's... If I am not, I miss the point of my life. I miss what being human is for me[58]."

The young people seem to assume people have freedom of choice. Or, do they assume that moral choices are determined and therefore people really cannot be held responsible for their action? Do they assume that all actions are determined by outside forces such as heredity, culture, or events? For them there is no conflict of duty; people simply are free to take one action or another. They may experience a conflict of preferences but not a conflict of duties. The young people probably would agree that beliefs, attitudes, feelings, and emotions are mental states and therefore cannot be judged to be right or wrong. A person cannot cease to have a particular mental state such as a particular feeling or emotion by choosing not to have it. Maybe they feel that moral choices are also mental states. As you can see, the personal view held by the young people raises many questions.

Conversation about duty - Mae and Bill

As I mentioned earlier, the purpose of the hypothetical conversations is to observe the use of the concepts presented in the Principled Thinking Model through thought experiments to see how the concepts might be used in ordinary conversation. The hypothetical conversations capture the use of the concepts of the five categories of the Principled Thinking Model: duty, rights, motive, desert and justice. These kinds of conversations are not that uncommon.[59]

Browse through the following conversation between the two hypothetical teachers, Mae and Bill, who teach 9th graders at Middletown Middle School. Both are taking their final courses towards their M. Ed. and are quite eager to push an argument as far as they can by challenging each other on different issues. They are not always on opposite sides of each other; they simply challenge each other's assertions. Mae, an English teacher for the past four years, has traveled the world and is planning to get married. Bill, a twelve year History teacher, is married and lives with his wife and one child.

Both have read the article, *If it feels right*, in the *New York* Times[60] by David Brooks where he reviewed a controversial Study about how young people in 2008 answered questions about right and wrong. Mae and Bill were troubled by the young people's response to questions about right and wrong and moral dilemmas. Both seem to agree with the conclusion drawn by Brooks when he maintained that people need categories and concepts to answer questions about right and wrong. During their lunch hour, they would get into spirited discussions. Here is their discussion about *duty*.

Immediately, they disagreed on whether all references to duties raise moral issues. Bill asserted, "Every reference to duties involves a moral sense."

"Not so quick," said Mae. "The term, wrong, is used in the moral sense in this statement: 'It is wrong for children to pick on the new classmate.' On the other hand, the term is used in a non-moral sense in this statement: 'He gave the wrong answer to that math question."

Bill had to concede to this distinction. At the same time, he added, "If it is a person's duty to do something, then the act of doing it is morally right, and it would be wrong not to do it."

"Before we get too far into our arguments about *duty*, we need to be clear about what is meant by 'doing one's duty," cautioned Mae.

"That's easy," retorted Bill. "It simply means a person follows whatever is his or her duty to do. People should simply follow whatever duty has been assigned to them."

"Really?" asked Mae. "Does it not matter whether a person actually wants to do what is his duty to do?"

"Well, maybe," admitted Bill.

"And," Mae added, "what if someone wants to do his duty *only* if it's the right thing to do?"

Bill had to concede again. He had been too quick to accept a simple meaning of *wanting to do one's duty*.

Mae raised a new question, "If an act is morally right, is it a person's duty to do it?"

"Not necessarily," Bill replied. "Just because it may be morally right for you to offer to cover my recess duty does not mean that it is your duty to do it."

Mae agreed and came up with another question, "Is doing one's duty something a person should do even though the person does not want to do it, in fact, objects to doing it?"

"Of course," Bill responded. "It is my duty to pay my taxes even though I don't want to pay taxes. Some teachers may like to do recess duty in order to relate to students more informally; others may not like to do it. Yet, teachers should do recess duty if it is their duty. If something is your duty, then you are obligated to do it. One follows from the other. In other words, if something is your obligation to do, then you should do it."

Mae was uncomfortable with Bill's use of the words duty and obligation interchangeably. She felt there is a difference. She pointed out to Bill, "You can put a person under an obligation but not under a duty. Obligations tend to be incurred as the result of something a person has done. The obligation *to keep ones promise* follows from the fact that a person made a promise. Duties, on the other hand, are assigned regardless of whether a person wants to do them or not."

Bill thought of a new twist on the issue of having a duty, "If someone was not a qualified teacher, would he have a duty to teach? Surely, a person does not have a duty to do what he cannot do."

"I guess not. What about acts done beyond the call of duty?" asked Mae.

To which Bill replied, "People consider such acts as right acts. Rescuing a drowning child is considered a heroic act or going beyond the call of duty."

Bill shifted the discussion to what he felt are more fundamental issues. He posed this question, "Are there degrees of being right as well as degrees of being wrong?"

Mae promptly pointed out that the answer to the first part of this question is obvious, "There are no degrees of being right. An act is either right or not. To assert that it is right to be fair to children cannot be half right or partly right or very right. It's simply right."

However, Bill maintained there are degrees of being wrong. He explained it this way, "One act can be more seriously wrong than another. It is considered, by most people, to be more seriously wrong to cheat on an exam than to copying a friend's answers for an assignment. Both are considered wrong but not to the same degree. A person would be punished more severely for cheating on an exam."

Bill raised another perplexing question, '"Does it follow from the fact that an act is right that not doing it is wrong?"

"I'm not sure," replied Mae.

So Bill ventured to answer his own question, "It may be wrong not to do the act and it need not be wrong. If it is a teacher's duty to do hallway supervision during the lunch hour, it is right for the teacher to do it and wrong not to do it. On the other hand, it may be right for a teacher to volunteer to coach students on the debating team, but it does not follow that it is wrong not to volunteer as a coach."

Mae wondered out loud, "Are there no morally indifferent acts?" She added, "To argue that there are no morally indifferent acts seems contrary to common sense. Some actions are neither right nor wrong; they are morally indifferent."

"You are right to point that out," maintained Bill. "As I said earlier, even though it may be right to serve as coach for a debating team, it does not follow that it is wrong not to coach. I consider this to be a morally indifferent act."

Mae followed up with what appeared to be a tricky statement, "Right and wrong are not contradictory terms; they are contrary terms."

Bill asked what she meant by this distinction.

"Actually," Mae replied, "this is not a trick statement. *Contradictory* means that both cannot be true … an act cannot be both right and wrong. Mocking a new immigrant student cannot be both, right and wrong."

"I get it," said Bill. "And," he added, "*contrary* refers to opposites or being opposed to each other. Right actions and wrong actions are opposites. That makes them contrary terms."

Mae raised the famous issue, "Ought implies can".

"So what is that supposed to mean?" asked Bill. "It seems obvious to me that if someone expects me to do something, I must be able to do it. Otherwise, I should not be expected to do it!"

"I have to agree with you," replied Mae.

Bill was interested in more practical issues. So he asked, "What if my friend, John, got involved in a collision with another car because he had been drinking to the point where he was not in my right mind? Should he be held responsible for his action?"

"Of course," maintained Mae. "He created the situation of not being in his right mind. That's why he should be held responsible."

"Not to be outdone, Bill asked, "What if he had not gotten involved in an accident with his car, would it have been wrong for him to have been drinking till he was no longer in his right mind?" Bill seemed to give John a pass.

Mae claimed, "John was wrong because he was not in his right mind due to his own action; he drank too much alcohol. As for the situation where he had been drinking and driving but did not get involved in an accident, I don't know."

"What about acting from a fit of anger? Is that wrong?" asked Mae. "What if the fit of anger is brought on by a malfunctioning of a gland or the brain?" She was quick to respond to the later by insisting, "If a person has a malfunctioning brain and consequently has lost control over his circumstance, he should not be held responsible for his action."

"On the other hand," Bill pointed out, "If the fit of anger is brought on by something a person could have influenced, he should be held responsible for his action in a fit of anger."

As part of their free flow conversation, Mae changed the discussion by raising the controversial issue of freedom of will vs. determinism by asking, "Do people have freedom of will?" Replying to her own question, she insisted, "The answer to this question has to be *yes*. Without this freedom to make moral judgments, a person should not be held responsible for what he did."

Bill looked at this issue from the perspective of determinism and maintained, "All events have causes.'"

That raised a further question for Mae, "Is choosing determined or does it have a cause?" To which she quickly added, "If choosing is not caused, would it not be like a bolt out of the blue?"

Bill fired back, "If that were so, how can a person be held responsible for what he chooses? If choices have no causes they would be inexplicable."

Mae was confused by Bill's explanation. "How can freedom of the will include determinism?" she asked.

Bill suggested, "Maybe freedom of will seems to refer to choices determined by reasons rather than by causes."

"But reasons may be just another set of causes!" retorted Mae.

In the end, both agreed that even if the distinction between causes and reasons could be established, they were not certain that they could resolve the problem of freedom of will vs. determinism. This was an intractable problem for them. At the same time, they felt compelled to assume that most people are responsible for their action at least some of the time.

Realizing that they had run out of time, Mae quickly raised one more question, "Can a person have a conflict of duties?"

"That is actually not possible," Bill maintained. "Since a person cannot do conflicting duties, he cannot have an actual conflict of duties."

Before Mae could respond, Bill insisted on one more question as well, a question which had bothered him for a long time, "Can beliefs, attitudes, feelings, and emotions be judged to be morally right or wrong?"

Mae surprised Bill with her elaborate response when she said, "I think beliefs, attitudes, feelings, and emotions are mental states. A person cannot cease to have a particular mental state such as a particular feeling or emotion by choosing not to have it. That's why they should not be judged to be right or wrong."

"I get it," responded Bill. "A person cannot arbitrarily cease to have a certain attitude. The same applies to thinking certain thoughts. A person cannot prevent a certain thought from crossing his mind." Suddenly, Bill remembered what his mother used to say, "My mother used to remind me that I cannot prevent a bird from flying over my head, but, I don't have to let it build a nest in my hair."

"I wonder why your mother used to say that to you?" mused Mae.

It was time for Mae and Bill to return to their afternoon classes.

Next day ...

When Bill and Mae sat down for their lunch break the next day, Mae picked up on their conversation by asking, "So how would our discussion yesterday differ from the views expressed by the young people as viewed by Brooks? In some ways, it doesn't seem that different," Mae continued. "The young people would agree with the non-moral or descriptive sense but not so much the moral sense. I am currently reading a recent book by Brooks, *Road to Character*, where he maintains that they trust themselves and distrust authority figures." Mae rambled on with a few more questions, "Do they accept that people have obligations? Do they honor an obligation to keep ones promise or is that also strictly a matter of personal choice?"

"I'm not certain that they do, except for rape and murder," observed Bill. "Imagine believing that you are doing right because you feel harmonious inside! Then any and all acts could be morally indifferent acts!"

"You are right," added Mae "For them, no external conditions need to be met for an action to be right or wrong. I guess there is no such thing as a morally right action for them when your personal feelings are the best guide for what is right and wrong."

I can't believe," says Bill, "that anyone could claim that one's desires are like an inner voice for what is right and true. How can you know you are doing the right thing whenever you feel good inside?"

"Do they believe that *ought* implies *can*?" asked Mae.

"I don't think that matters to them," replied Bill. "Since they do not accept any responsibilities, *ought* is quite meaningless for them."

Mae continued with her philosophical musings by asking, "Do they assume that people have freedom of choice? Or do they assume that all action is determined by outside forces such as heredity, culture, or events?"

No comments from Bill ... this issue was not at all clear to him. He realized that Mae is more knowledgeable about how morality intersects with social justice.

Bill observed that he could agree with the young people on one issue. As he put it, "I agree with the young people that beliefs, attitudes, feelings, and emotions are mental states and therefore should not be judged to be right or wrong."

"You are right," added Mae. "One cannot cease to have a particular feeling or emotion by choosing not to have it. When I feel sad about my sister, who died in a horrific motorcycle accident, I cannot stop that feeling. Nor can I avoid the feeling of anger towards the person who caused the accident."

Although they felt exhausted, they also felt rejuvenated by the stimulating discussion. The lunch hour had passed in a flash.

Moral thinking does not only take into account whether a person has a *duty*, it also takes into account the *rights* of the person who contemplated or consummated an act. In the next Chapter, I review the concepts related to the *rights* people have.

Chapter 6
Rights

Conceptual Framework

Most people tire quickly when someone keeps reminding them of their duties or responsibilities. Before long, they shift the conversation to their rights. In other words, we tend to be quite defensive about our rights and object to being reminded of our duties.

This Chapter is focused on the concepts we use when we assert our *rights*. Here are a few questions that come to mind:
- What does it mean to say that 'John has a claim to X'?
- How do we distinguish moral rights from legal rights?
- What does it mean to have a prerogative?
- Is it true that for every duty a person has a corresponding right?
- Is it the case that to every right there is a correlative duty?

This class of terms, for which the word *rights* is a representative term, includes many words which have a similar meaning. These include:

> claim, prerogative, justified, warranted, entitled, give, bestow, lend,, own, belong, have, own, his, hers, yours, mine, property, sell, purchase, buy, ownership, inherit, confer, legitimate, illegitimate, earn, authority[61]

Key words

The word, *rights*, introduces the notion of someone *having a right* to do something or *having a right to something*. This sense of the word *rights* makes reference to people's objects of interest. It refers to what a person would like to have, prefer, wish for or want. On the other hand, object of disinterest refers to what a person may be averse to, not want, avoid, escape from or does not wish for. Reference to objects of interest also introduces an element of motives which are discussed in Chapter 7.

People frequently make a distinction between *human rights* and *legal rights*. As I have mentioned before, when a right is claimed to be a moral right, it is a right which people claim they have as human beings. Hence, these rights are referred to as human rights. Legal rights refers to rights which people have in law. A human right can be enshrined in law and become a legal right. However, a human right is a right even when it is not established as a legal right. For example, freedom of speech is regarded a human right. It continues to be a human right whether or not it was legislated as a legal right. If it became a legal right in a particular country, it would be both a human right and a legal right in that country.

Some terms are interchangeable. The terms *to be entitled* and *to be warranted* basically have the same meaning. To say that John is entitled to an award is to say that John has a right to the award. To say that a reward was not warranted for Jim's performance is to say that Jim did not have a right to receive the award.

Key ideas

The most basic concept of the category, *rights*, is *object of interest*. In the statement 'John has a right to do X', *right* is used in the moral sense as in statements about human rights found in documents such as the Canadian Bill of Rights and the United Nations Declaration of the Rights of Man. These documents have been drafted to identify, advocate, and protect people's rights or objects of interest.

What does it mean to *have a right to an object of interest*? It means that it is not wrong for a person to pursue it; nor would it be wrong for the person not to pursue it. It would be wrong for someone else to prevent a person from pursuing an object of interest if he or she has a right to it. For example, if Mary has the right to read a certain novel, it is not wrong for her to read it. Mary would be free to read it or not. It would be wrong for someone to prevent her from reading it. Others would have a duty not to prevent her from reading it. If Mary would prefer not to read the novel, it would not be right to compel her to read it.

For 'X' to be a *right*, it must be an object of interest, either actual or potential. People demand rights and are frequently willing to protect and defend their rights. An infringement of rights sometimes results in anger.

Although it would be wrong for anyone to prevent a person from having or enjoying objects of interest if it is a right, it does not follow that a person has a right to pursue all of his objects of interests. For example, suppose a person has a right to exercise freedom of speech, it would be wrong for someone to prevent a person from exercising freedom of speech. On the other hand, it would be wrong for a teacher not to interfere when several children exercise their freedom of speech by teasing a new child in school.

We use the term *authority* frequently in every day conversation. So, let me explain how we use it in the moral and non-moral sense. In the moral sense, we say a captain of a soccer team has the authority or right to give instructions. In the formal institutional sense, it refers to Parliament's right to make laws, a judge's right to pronounce a sentence, or a general's right to command an army. Some people have the authority to confer to others a *right* to do something. For example, a principal can authorize or confer upon the secretary of a school the *right* to open the school mail.

The word *authority* is used in a non-moral or descriptive sense in, "He is a person of authority on migratory birds." The word *authority* in this case is used in the descriptive sense to refer to a person who is regarded as being knowledgeable in a particular area. The term, *legitimate*, sometimes is used in a moral sense although it is more often used in a legal sense.

To say "John set up a legitimate research centre" is to say that John had a right to set up the centre. On the other hand, to say that "Bill's activities are illegitimate" means that he does not have the legal right or moral right (or both) to do them.

There are a few more commonly used terms which also convey a moral sense of right. One of the basic terms, at least in the Western culture, is *ownership* which means the right to use, enjoy or dispose of something. The meaning of this word becomes clear when it is contrasted with the term *possession*. To say that "John possesses X" is to say that John has the actual power to use, enjoy, and dispose of X. For example, a thief, who has stolen a car, is in possession of a stolen vehicle and therefore is in a position to use the vehicle for whatever purpose he chooses. He might choose to use it to leave the country, to sell it for quick cash or for some other purpose. However, people would not say that he owns the car or that it belongs to him. Should the true owner of the car accidentally meet up with the thief who stole the car, the owner, no doubt, would say to the thief, "The car belongs to me!" or "That is my car, not yours!"

The term *ownership* introduces a few more terms such as *belong* and *possessive personal pronouns* like *my* and *yours*. The following vignette illustrates how a group of terms related to ownership work together. Suppose the owner of a car reported to the police that his vehicle has been stolen and suppose the police apprehended the thief. He would have to appear in court to face the criminal charge of theft. He would be charged with depriving the true owner of his personal property. The reference to *property* refers to the fact that the car is owned by a certain person even though he may temporarily have lost possession of it. Although the thief possessed the car he did not own it. Upon further questioning by a judge, the owner would report that he had not given the car to the alleged thief. In other words, the owner had not transferred his right to the car to the alleged thief, which means that the owner had not agreed to or arranged for a transfer of his ownership rights to the alleged thief.

If a judge had inquired into how the owner came to acquire ownership of the vehicle in question, the owner would have produced documentation verifying his ownership of the vehicle.

Should the alleged thief be a teenager, he might claim that there is no cause for any legal hassle because he did not mean to do any harm. The owner probably would retort, with indignation, that as the owner of the car, he has the prerogative of determining who may drive his car. This vignette illustrates how the concepts related to ownership work together in the legal and moral sense. To ignore the difference between ownership and possession could lead to confusing consequences.

Finally, let me add a few more common terms related to rights that are used in the moral and the descriptive sense. The word *have* can be used in both ways. *I have a car* can mean that I own a car or I possess a car. The word *earn* also takes on different meanings in different statements. It can be used descriptively in a factual statement like "He earns $300.00 a week." It can also mean acquiring a right to a particular position by working for it as in "She really earned that position." However, *I have a brownish complexion* does not really refer to ownership or possession but describes a certain personal feature.

Rights must be distinguished from duties. As I mentioned above, duties are regarded as being burdensome or onerous whereas rights are sought after and defended. This distinction is reflected in the fact that a person is sometimes deprived of his rights but relieved of his duties. For example, In 1970, the Prime Minister of Canada, Pierre Elliot Trudeau, invoked the War Measures Act which suspended basic civil rights and liberties for all Canadians. The Act, passed in 1914, sets out the general *obligations* [duties] of the government for the safety and security of individuals. In 1988 the Act was repealed and replaced by the Emergency Act to ensure that the War Measures Act would not infringe on the *rights* of Canadians.

The *difference between rights and a duty* is illustrated by the following role of a journalist. A journalist has the human right of freedom of speech, and, as a social critic for a newspaper syndicate, she may also have a duty to exercise her freedom of speech. The human right does not establish that the journalist has a duty to exercise it. However, if she has a duty to exercise freedom of speech as a reporter, she also has a right to exercise it. In short, a person may *have a right* as well as a *duty*.

To say that 'John has a claim to X is to say that there are *some reasons to believe that John has a right* to X. Several people may maintain that they have a claim to X. However, a person has a right to it only if he has *sound reasons* for making his claim. For example, several people may claim a missing book which was found but only the person who has sound reasons for making his claim has a right to the book.

I need to draw attention to the difference between *having a claim to X* and *"justifying a right* to X." *Having a claim to X* is to say that there are sound reasons to believe that a person has a right to X, but, *to justify a right to X* is to say that there are sufficient reasons for a person to have a right to X. For example, for John to claim a right to a particular lost book, he must produce a justification (sufficient reasons) for making his claim.

The relationship between *having rights* and *having a duty* raises a few more issues. First, *do rights and duties correspond?* This question raises two more questions:

1. If John Doe has a right then in virtue of his having that right, does he have a certain duty?
2. If John has a duty then in virtue of his having that duty, does he have a certain right?

Let me rephrase the first question: *"Is it true that for every right, a person has a corresponding duty?"* At first glance, it would seem that for every right there is a corresponding duty. For example, if John Doe has a right to free speech then in virtue of his having that right, does he have a duty to acknowledge this right for others? Consider this situation. A person, who has the right to marry and have children, would seem to have the corresponding duty of looking after those children. However, this example of *corresponding duty* has exceptions. In a number of societies, arrangements are made for social institutions to assist in looking after the children or even to assume full responsibility for raising the children.

Second, we recognize that children have rights (though not necessarily civil rights), but they do not necessarily have corresponding duties. It could be argued that children have potential corresponding duties. In other words, children will have to assume certain duties as soon as they have acquired the ability to assume responsibility for their action. In summary, the correspondence between rights and duties does not seem to be clear cut.

Let's look at the reverse question: *"Is it true that for every duty, a person has a corresponding right?"* The right would have to be something other than the right to do ones duty. For example, if it is your duty to keep promises, then you have a right to expect it of others. Does a person have a right to expect it of all others, including young children who may not be able to keep promises because they have not developed the cognitive ability to understand promises? Not necessarily. Second, if you have the duty to obey, what *corresponding* right do you have? Some people might argue that the obedient person has a right to expect recognition or reward. However, recognition or rewards usually are given only in situations where a person was obedient under exceptional circumstances.

Here is another example: "What are the *corresponding rights* to the duty referred to in the statement, "We have a duty to work for the benefit of mankind." Suppose Albert Schweitzer felt it was his duty to provide medical services to indigenous people living in the jungles of Africa. What would be Schweitzer's corresponding right? Would he have a right to a fully equipped and staffed hospital? The answer is not immediately clear. In short the correspondence between duties and rights seems subject to each situation.

I conclude that *it cannot be established that duties and rights correspond* though I acknowledge that some plausible correspondence is conceivable.

The second major problem raised about the relationship between rights and duties is: *"Are rights and duties correlative?"* This raises the following questions:

1. If John has a certain duty then in virtue of his having that duty, does someone have a certain right?

2. If John has a certain right, then in virtue of his having that certain right, does someone have a certain duty?

The answer to the first of these two questions is as uncertain as were the answers to the questions raised concerning the correspondence of rights and duties. It is not clear why there is a *correlative* connection between the duty and the rights. Suppose it is John's duty to help the poor. It does not follow that any poor person has the right to go up to John and demand financial assistance. John may have elected to meet his duty to help the poor through donations to a non-profit organization. In other words, it is not clear that to every duty there is a correlative right.

Let's look at the converse question: "*Is it the case that to every right there is a correlative duty?*" The answer to this question is contained in the meaning of the concept of *having a right* discussed earlier in this section. It was pointed out that to every right a person has, someone else has a duty. For John to have a right to X, it is the duty of everyone not to deny John this right. The duty of everyone else towards the person who has a right is a part of the meaning of *having a right*. Hence, *to every right there is a correlative duty* is analytically true. To deny it would be contradictory.

It would appear that only one of the questions raised concerning the relationship between having a right and having a duty can be answered conclusively. That is the question concerning the correlativity of rights and duties. As I explained above, *to every right there is a correlative duty* is analytically true.

Let me raise another debatable question about rights: *Do animals have rights?* Many people would claim that animals do not have rights but that they should be treated humanely. They would maintain that people have a duty to treat animals humanely.

This question raises a broader issue: If for someone/something to have a right, he/it must be a moral person, or a potential moral person. How might this condition apply to animals? In other words, how can animals be *moral persons*? The most basic right of animals, if they have any, would be the right to live which raises many questions to which there are conflicting views. Here are some of the questions:

(a) Is it wrong to kill a tiger for its fur? Is it right if the fur is required to keep people warm in certain circumstances?
(b) Is it right to kill a tiger to obtain a decorative rug (i.e., for aesthetic reasons)?
(c) Is it wrong to kill an animal that is on the verge of becoming extinct?
(d) Is it wrong to kill baby seals?
(e) Is it more seriously wrong to kill some members of the animal kingdom than others? If so, how should the following be categorized: mosquito, pheasant, calf, alligator, buffalo, rabbit?

These questions demonstrate the complexity of the term *rights* and how it is used to make moral judgments. The topic of animal rights is important because scholars like Yuval Harari[23] remind us that humans share a common heritage with animals. Therefore, we should recognize that rights apply not only to homo sapiens but also to animals.

We have seen in this Chapter how important *rights* are for making moral judgments. So many every-day situations involve *rights*. It is interesting to observe that many common words like *have*, which usually are not regarded as moral terms, include a moral sense.

Figure 6 identifies questions about *rights* that are addressed in this Chapter.

Questions about Rights
1. What is meant by the statement, John has a right to X?
2. How can punishment be a right when it is clearly regarded as an object of disinterest?
3. How are actual objects of interest different from potential objects of interest?
4. How are moral rights different from legal rights?
5. What does it mean to say that *John has a claim to X*?
6. Does *to be entitled* mean the same as *to be warranted*?
7. Is the word *legitimate* also used in a moral sense?
8. How does *ownership* differ from *possession*?
9. Does the word *belong* mean the same as *ownership*?
10. What does it mean to have a *prerogative*?
11. What are some of the different ways we use the word *have*?
12. What are some different ways we use the word *earn*?
13. Is it true that for every duty a person has a *corresponding* right?
14. Is it true that for every right a person has a *corresponding* duty?
15. Is it the case that for every right there is a *correlative* duty?
16. Is it the case that for every duty there is a *correlative* right?
17. Do animals have *rights*?

Figure 6: Rights

Young people's view of rights

The youth in the study reviewed by Brooks do not agree for the most part with the concept of *rights* (having a right to do something or having a right to something) presented in this book. For them, objects of interest simply refers to "It's personal ... it's up to the individual." Brooks elaborates on this view in *The Road to Character* by paraphrasing what Rabbi Joseph Soloveitchik describes in *Lonely Man of* Faith[62] as the *Adam* 1 side of nature. Here is what Brooks has to say, "Adam 1 lives by a straightforward utilitarian logic. It's the logic of economics. Input leads to output. Effort leads to reward. Practice makes perfect. Pursue self-interest. Maximize your utility. Impress the world[63]."

Brooks adds that young people maintain that they "go through life as a self-contained unit, coolly weighing risks and rewards and looking out for your own interests[64]." Rights appear to be a matter of looking after your own interests.

If *having a right* is personal then a person has a right to pursue any and all of his objects of interests. The young people probably would agree with the statement: "Rights are those objects of interest which it would be wrong for anyone to prevent a person from having or enjoying[65]."

Brooks makes an interesting historical observation about the young people's views of having a right to objects of interest. He observes, "[Putting] more emphasis on pride and self esteem had many positive effects; it helped correct some deep social injustices. Up until those years, many social groups, notably women, minorities and the poor had received messages of inferiority and humiliation. The culture of self-esteem encouraged members of these oppressed groups to believe in themselves, and to raise their sites and aspirations[66]."

The young people probably would agree with the statement: For someone to have a right to do X, X must be an *object of interest*. It certainly would not include *objects of disinterest*. Brooks describes it this way: "[to the extent that a person] can be freely in touch with his valuing process in himself, he will behave in ways that are self-enhancing[67]." The focus of rights is on the self, not on others.

The young people distinguish moral rights from legal rights. Moral rights for them are personal or *up to the individual*, whereas legal rights refer to legislated rights. Brooks adds a positive note on their view of human rights, "The emphasis on self-actualization and self-esteem gave millions of women a language to articulate and cultivate self-assertion, strength, and identity[68]." In other words, human rights can offer great personal strength and identity.

The young people do not make a clear distinction between *duties* and *rights*. They claim that both are personal or up to the individual. However, if it is unclear from one moment to the next whether someone has a duty and/or a right, the distinction between them is unclear. They are both determined by the same criteria, *It's up to the individual*. Both are determined by whatever a person wants or desires.

The words *claim* and *justify* present a problem for the young people. If having a right is simply personal or up to the individual, how can that viewpoint be reconciled with having sufficient reasons to show or demonstrate that a person has a right to something? Brooks puts another spin on *justifying* when he refers to Dr. Seuss' 1990 book, *Oh, the Places You'll Go!*[69], which is about a boy who is reminded that he has all these amazing talents and gifts and enjoys ultimate freedom to choose his life. The boy is reminded that "his life is about fulfilling his own desires[70]," In this case, rights are equated with desires; not with providing sufficient reasons to justify that a person has a right to something.

The young people's view of authority seems to break down. If moral choices are just a matter of individual taste, how can Parliament have a right to make laws for others, a judge have a right to pronounce a sentence, or a general have a right to command his army? Quoting the philosopher, Charles Taylor, Brooks says young people today claim their mindset "is based on the romantic idea that each of us has a Golden Figure in the core of our self. There is an innately good True Self, which can be trusted, consulted, and gotten in touch with[71]." In other words,

Charles Taylor maintains that your personal feelings are the best guide for what is right and wrong.

The young people would have a problem with the term *legitimate*. It seems meaningless to say that *to be legitimate* means someone has a right to do something or has a right to something when rights simply refers to "It's personal, ... It's up to the individual." It follows that a person can do whatever he or she wants to do.

The concept of *ownership* seems to present a problem for young people according to Brooks when *ownership* refers to the right to use, enjoy or dispose of something which a person owns. No two persons might agree on who owns or possesses anything. They fail to distinguish between ownership and possession in that both terms seem to refer to possessing an object of interest.

Brooks summarizes the young people's view of rights and duties this way: "Your personal feelings are the best guide for what is right and wrong. In this ethos, the self is to be trusted, not doubted. Your desires are like inner oracles for what is right and true. You know you are doing the right thing when you feel good inside. The valid rules of life are those you make or accept for yourself and that feel right for you[72]." Hence, correspondence between rights and duties is irrelevant. There is no necessary correspondence between what constitutes a duty or a right because every individual is free to decide for him or herself what constitutes a *duty* or a *right*.

The question of whether *duties* and *rights* are *correlative* is quite simple for the young people who claim that moral choices are just a matter of individual taste. Every individual has to decide for himself what constitutes a duty and a right. Consequently, rights and duties are not correlative. Brooks quotes celebrity chef Mario Batali who advised graduates to follow "your own truth, expressed consistently by you[73]."

The young people probably would agree that the statement, *to every right there is a correlative duty is analytically true*, because they probably respect an analytic truth. They would agree that for John Doe to have a right, it is everyone's duty not to deny him that right. In other words, it is meaningless to say that John Doe has a right if nobody has a duty to defend his right. Everyone's duty not to deny him that right is inherent in *John Doe has a right*.

According to Brooks, young people probably would agree with the following concepts about *rights* presented in this book:

- For John to have a right to do X, X must be an object of interest, either actual or potential.
- Rights are those objects of interest which it would be wrong for anyone to prevent a person from having or enjoying.
- Distinguish moral rights from legal rights.
- It is analytically true to say that *to every right there is a correlative duty*.

The young people depart from the view of rights presented in this book in several areas.

- They make an unclear distinction between duties and rights. They claim that both are personal or up to the individual. It is unclear from one moment to the next whether someone has a duty and/or a right because both are determined by the same criteria, *It's up to the individual*. Hence, the use of these categories is meaningless.
- If having a right is personal or up to the individual, how can that be reconciled with having sufficient reasons to show or justify that a person has a right to something?

Conversation about rights - Mae and Bill

Let's return to the conversation between Bill and Mae whom we met in a conversation about *duty*. After a few pleasantries about the courses they were taking to complete their Masters requirements, Bill referred to an article in the local newspaper about a young person, Mary, who defended her right to smoke a joint in a local park.

When Bill defended Mary's right, Mae retorted, "What do you mean by having a right?"

Bill replied, "Rights refers to having a right to an object of interest."

Not satisfied with Bill's simple response, Mae asked, "What does it mean to have a right to an object of interest?"

Now Bill is struggling ... it will not be easy to answer Mae's question. He tried, "Having a right means that it is not wrong for a person to pursue a specific interest; nor would it be wrong not to pursue it."

"Surely I would have a right to stop Mary from smoking a joint in a public park!" retorted Mae.

"It would be wrong to prevent Mary from smoking a joint in a public park if it is her right to do so," stressed Bill. "She would be free to smoke or not to smoke. In fact, other people, including yourself, would have a duty not to prevent her from smoking. However, if smoking a joint in a public park was not something Mary wants to do, it would not be right to compel her to do it."

Mae raised the bar by asking, "Does it follow that a person has a right to pursue all of his or her interests?"

Bill winced and replied, "Of course not. If it would not be wrong to light up a joint in a public park, Mary would have a right to do so. On the other hand, if it would be wrong to smoke a joint in a public park, she would not have a right to do so." Realizing that he probably had ventured into the distinction between legal and human rights, Bill observed, "People frequently make a distinction between human rights and legal rights."

Mae asked, "So what is the distinction?"

Without hesitation Bill replied, "When a right is claimed to be a human right, it is a right which people claim they have as human beings. Legal rights refers to rights which people have in law."

Mae was on a roll; so she pummeled Bill with a series of questions, "Can a *human right* become a *legal right*? Is a human right a right even when it is not a legal right? Are all legal rights also human rights?"

"Where do I begin?" Bill thought to himself. He responded, "A human right is regarded a right even when it is not a legal right. For example, freedom of speech is regarded a human right. It would continue to be a human right whether or not it was legislated to become a legal right. If it became a legal right in a country, it would be both a human right and a legal right."

Mae's thoughts shifted to what they had discussed about duties previously. She was curious about the relationship between duties and rights. So, she asked, "What do you think is the relationship between duties and rights?"

Bill was ready for this question; he had wondered about the relationship as well. So, he said, "A person can be deprived of his legal rights but relieved of his duties as in being dismissed at work. At the same time, a person may have a right as well as a duty," continued Bill. "As a math teacher, I have the responsibility of instructing and coaching the students in my classes. At the same time, I have the right to preparation time to create my lessons. Furthermore, I have the responsibility to grade my students' work in a timely manner and a right to paid recreation time during the school year. If I fail to meet my responsibilities, I could be relieved on my teaching contract and so lose my paid recreation time.

Mae was still troubled by what constitutes a right. So she asked again, "What does it mean to say that Mary has a right to an object of interest, say, smoking a joint in a public park?"

Bill maintained, "Mary has to have some reasons for making the claim."

"So might someone else offer reasons for not allowing Mae to smoke a joint in a park," retorted Mae.

Bill tightened his explanation, "A person would have to give sound reasons to make the claim."

Mae was still perplexed because she is wondering about the difference between having sound reasons for claiming a right and justifying a right.

So, she asked, "What is the difference between *having a right* and *justifying a right?*

Bill thought for a moment; then offered this explanation, "*Having a claim to a right* is to say that there are sound reasons for claiming a right. I'm not sure how that is different from justifying a right."

Mae was disappointed with Bill's failure to point out the difference; she had a problem with the distinction as well.

Bill was still troubled about the relationship between *having a duty* and *having rights*. So he asked, "Is it true that for every right, a person has a corresponding duty?"

Mae had to think about this question for a while before she responded, "At first glance, it would seem to me that for every right a person has a corresponding duty. For example, if Mary has the right to smoke pot in a public place, it would seem to me that she has a corresponding duty not to cause harm to others with her smoking. However, it might be difficult sometimes to determine whether an act, like smoking pot, harms others in specific situations. Hence, the correspondence between rights and duties is not clear cut to me."

Bill was impressed and waited for an equally incisive explanation for the converse question, "Is it true that for every duty a person has a corresponding right?" How would Mae respond to this question, he wondered.

Mae came up with another perceptive response, "Of course, the right would have to be something other than the right to do ones duty. That would suggest a direct correspondence. Let me try another situation. Earlier I said that everyone has a duty not to harm others. Does it follow that therefore Mary has a right to smoke pot in public places provided she does not cause harm to others? Not necessarily. There may be several reasons why people should not be allowed to smoke pot in public places. Hence, it seems to me there is no direct correspondence between specific duties and rights.

Bill was not satisfied with Mae's explanation. So he asked, "If I have a duty to obey, what corresponding right do I have? Surely, if I have a duty to obey, I must have some rights!"

"What rights are you thinking of?" asked Mae.

"My human rights must not be violated. I must be able to do what I am required to do. I may need some training to prepare me to fulfill my duties."

Mae had to agree with Bill on this issue.

Hence, both concluded that it cannot be established whether duties and rights correspond though they acknowledge that some plausible correspondence is conceivable. In some situations they correspond and some they do not.

Mae thought of another difficult question. So she asked, "Is it true that for every *duty*, someone has a *correlative right*?"

Bill replied, "It is not clear to me whether for every duty there is a correlative right. Of course, if a person has a duty to do X, he must have the right to do X; otherwise it could not be his duty. On the other hand, just because it is everyone's duty not to harm others does not deny Mary the right to smoke pot which might or might not harm others in a public park. There is no absolute correlative relationship between duties and rights in this situation."

Mae asked the converse question, "For every right, is there is a correlative duty?"

Bill took a shot at this question, "The answer to this question is contained in the meaning of the concept of *having a right*. To every right a person has, someone else has a duty. For Mary to have a right to smoke pot in a public park, it is the duty of everyone else not to deny Mary that right. That's why I think that 'to every right there is a correlative duty'. I maintain it is analytically true."

"To deny it would be contradictory," confirmed Mae.

The conversation shifted to questions often raised to stir up emotional responses. Mae asked, "Do animals have rights?"

Bill responded with a personal view, "Many of us maintain that animals do not have rights but they should be treated humanely."

Mae added, "I believe that the most basic right of animals is the right to live."

Bill pointed out that this leaves many questions unanswered. He blurted out a number of questions that came to mind, "Is it wrong to kill a tiger for its fur? Is it right if the fur is required to keep people warm in certain circumstances? Is it right for someone to kill a tiger to obtain a decorative rug? Is it wrong to kill an animal which is on the verge of becoming extinct? Is it wrong to kill baby seals?"

Mae got Bill's point; so she added, "Is it more seriously wrong to kill some members of the animal kingdom than others? If so, how should we prioritize the following: mosquito, pheasant, calf, alligator, buffalo, and rabbit?"

Both knew there were no obviously clear answers to these questions; they were uncertain of animal's ability to perceive and respond to sensations of whatever kind - sight, hearing, touch, taste, or smell.

As they left to return to their classes, Mae observed, "It is interesting that many common words, which usually are not regarded as moral terms, seem to include a moral sense."

To which Bill added, "Many questions seem to defy definite answers."

A week later ...

When Bill and Mae resumed their conversation a week later during the lunch hour, they returned to the critique presented by Brooks in *The Road to Character*.

Bill asked, "Would the young people take a straightforward utilitarian view of looking out for their own interests?"

"Possibly," replied Mae. "They might also focus on the happiness for the greatest number of people."

To which Bill added this observation by Brooks, "For them it would be wrong for anyone to prevent a person from having or enjoying a right."

"There have been some positive outcomes from this focus," Mae reminded Bill. "Women, minorities and the poor, who traditionally were considered inferior and often were humiliated, have achieved a sense of self-esteem from this focus on universal rights."

Bill replied "I think you are referring to legal rights to be distinguished from human rights."

"Actually, Bill, I am referring to both legal and human rights," asserted Mae. Then she drew attention to another problem, "The young people do not make a clear distinction between duties and rights. Both are simply up to the individual. Both seem to be determined by whatever a person wants or desires."

To which Bill replied, "For them there is no necessary correspondence between what is a duty or a right because every individual is free to decide for himself about their duties and rights. Why would a person be asked to provide sound reasons to support a claim, when having a right is based simply on personal preferences?"

"Good question," Mae replied, "I suspect that the word *justify* presents no problem for them when rights seem to be equated with desires." She found that troubling. "They seem to believe that everyone seems to have a true self in their core which can be trusted."

This raised the question of authority for Bill, "How can Parliament have a right to make laws, a judge pronounce a sentence or a general command his army when rights are based on personal preferences?"

"Good question," replied Mae. "It makes no sense to me."

"How do they view the concept of ownership which to me means the right to use, enjoy or dispose of something," asked Bill. "It's so basic in our society."

Mae agreed and added, "The concept of ownership seems to present a problem for them. They do not seem to distinguish between ownership and possession in that both seem to describe the notion of possessing something."

"On the other hand," Bill added, "maybe they use ownership strictly in the legal sense of having the sole right and not in the moral sense."

With that, both agreed to continue their conversation the next time when both would be free of lunch duty.

Moral thinking does not only take into account whether a person has a *duty* and *rights*, it also takes into account the *motive* of the person who contemplated or consummated an act. In the next Chapter, I review the terms related to people's *motive* for doing right and/or wrong acts.

Chapter 7
Motive

Conceptual Framework

Have you ever been accused by a friend of imputing a motive for something he did which you disapproved of? Did you ever wonder why we impute motives? Are motives that important to us? I have imputed motives and felt awkward when I have been confronted about it. I recall asking my wife why she had not called me when her meeting was running later than planned. When she replied that she had called several times but nobody had answered the phone, I recalled that I had left my cell phone on the kitchen counter while I was in my study. I had imputed a motive, namely, she had not bothered to call.

We are driven by motives. They are reasons or emotions that drive our actions, often for personal gain. Some motives are morally good and some are not. In this Chapter, I identify the concepts we use when we are committed to act from a morally good motive in pursuit of justice and how that relates to doing one's duty.

I raise many questions about motives which are summarized in Figure 7 in this Chapter. Here are a few examples.
- What is a *morally good motive*?
- What if a person does an act which is actually wrong but he believes it to be right and he does it from a morally good motive?
- Are *compassion* and *love* examples of morally good motives?
- Is *morally bad* simply the converse of *morally good*?

- Does *morally bad* refer to the desire to do wrong for the sake of doing wrong?
- What is the *motive* of a person who is careless?

The representative words for this class are *morally good* and *virtue* as well as their converse *morally bad* and *vice*. Included in this class of terms are the following:

> moral excellence, evil, sinful, wicked, (nasty), wanton, nice, morally cleansed, ill repute, awful, corrupt, terrible, decadent, effete, criminal, ethical, unethical, moral, immoral, heinous, atrocious, (gross), depraved, nefarious, inequity, odious, hideous, (repugnant), vile, foul, degenerate, degraded, defiled, (demonic), (unholy), debased, debouched, angelic, upright, upstanding, noble, righteous, dutiful[74].

Key words

The concepts about *duty*, which are described in Chapter 5, refer to judgments of right and wrong without considering the motive of the person who did the act. However, judgments about right and wrong also include taking into account the motive of the person who contemplated or consummated an act. Hence, this class of terms adds a significant dimension to judgments about duties.

There are *good motives* besides the desire to do what is right or do one's duty, but they are not considered morally good motives. For example, *compassion* and *love* are considered good motives. Suppose a parent helps her daughter with her homework day after day out of love? Is she acting from a morally good motive? Not necessarily, let me explain.

Love is a motive from which a non-moral person could also act. Insofar that a moral person acts from this motive, she is no different from a non-moral person. If a non-moral person acted from the motive of love, the motive would not be regarded as a morally good motive because the non-moral person is not capable of distinguishing right from wrong, have the concepts of right and wrong or understands the meaning of right and wrong. If love cannot be judged to be a morally good motive for non-moral person, it should not be judged to be a morally good motive for a moral person. In short, love is a good motive, but not a morally good motive. Morally good motives are distinguished from good motives such as love, generosity, kindness, and friendship which sometimes are referred to as *naturally good motives*.

Not all virtues are *moral virtues*. For example, *wit* (i.e., quickness of thought) is regarded as an intellectual virtue but not a moral virtue. On the other hand, some virtues, like *truthfulness*, are regarded as moral virtues. It is a moral virtue because telling the truth is the right thing to do. It is regarded a moral virtue because it refers to a propensity, tendency or disposition to do what is the right thing to do. In short, a *moral virtue* is a disposition to do what is right from morally good motives. A *virtuous act* is a manifestation of a moral virtue.

Morally good and *virtuous* are not only applied to action and motives, but also to people. Is a *virtuous person* the same as a *morally good person*? This question distinguishes a disposition from actually doing something. As I pointed out before, *morally good* refers to the disposition of the person. A morally good person must have a consistent inclination to do virtuous acts like telling the truth, being friendly, or being generous. *Virtuous* refers to a person who is actually doing what is right. A virtuous person would resist, with persistence, the temptation to do wrong acts such as degrading other people, committing odious or dastardly deeds, or living a degenerate life.

When an *act is very bad, morally*, it is judged to be evil, atrocious, wicked, iniquitous, nefarious, fiendish, or demonic. *Wicked* applies to both the act and the person. *Nefarious* applies only to the act. *Heinous* expresses a strong disapproval of both, the act and the person. *Vile* or *foul* expresses a strong feeling of disgust. What makes an act morally worse is the degree of the seriousness of the wrong act. For example, it is more seriously wrong to murder a person than to steal a car.

Cynics do not believe that people ever act from morally good motives but act purely from a *motive of self-interest*. For example, when a teacher stays after school to help a student with his math, the cynic would maintain that the teacher does it from an ulterior motive of self-interest and not from a desire to do what is right. When John Doe pays regular visits to his ailing father in hospital, the cynic would suspect that John Doe is protecting his interests in an inheritance. The cynic would claim that he does not make regular visits just because he loves his father. When someone performs his duty faithfully, the cynic would argue that he does so for any number of ulterior motives such as wanting the approval of others, avoiding the disapproval of others, or fearing punishment. Acting from a motive of self-interest seems to be the only motive considered by a cynic.

Key ideas

There are certain conditions that must be fulfilled for an *act to be morally good*. As has been pointed out earlier, an *act must be right*. If John does an act which is clearly wrong, the act is not a morally good act. For example, prejudicial employment practices are not morally good acts because they are wrong. Second, the action must be done from a *morally good motive*. Suppose John helped a blind man cross the street so that the he would not have an accident. The reason given for helping the blind man is a morally good motive, namely, so that the blind man would not have an accident. The act would also strike most people as being the right thing to do. Hence, this course of action is regarded as a morally good act.

However, sometimes *a person does an act which is actually wrong, but he believes it to be right and he does it from a morally good motive*. Suppose a principal refuses to allow a student to be promoted because he believes that it is his duty to prevent students from being promoted when they have too many failing grades. It would not be a morally good act if the act itself is wrong even if the principal acted from a morally good motive. Suppose the principal is motivated to fail a student because the student is a trouble maker at school. The act would be wrong and his motive for failing the student would not be good and therefore his action to fail the student would not be morally good.

A *morally good motive* must meet two conditions. First, the person must *believe that a certain act is right* and second, the person must have a *desire to do what is right*. Just believing something is not a morally good motive. To say that "He did the right thing from a sense of duty" means that he believed it to be the right thing to do and he wanted to do his duty.

Wanting to do one's duty must be distinguished from *wanting to do one's duty because it is the right thing to do*. For example, suppose a teacher does lunch duty because he wants to comply with the lunch duty roster at his school. This teacher simply wants to do his duty. Suppose another teacher does her lunch duty because she wants to do the right thing for students who stay at school for lunch. She wants to make sure the students have a safe and pleasant place to eat lunch. This teacher does her duty because she is motivated to wanting to do the right thing. Probably, she would challenge her principal if he asked her to do something she felt was not the right thing to do.

A review of moral goodness suggests that there seem to be *levels of moral goodness*. The highest level of moral goodness is achieved by someone who would never do anything which is wrong and who would always do his duty or do the right thing because it is the right thing to do. This, no doubt, would have to serve as a hypothetical ideal since nobody is perfect. As we saw in the Introduction, the reasoning reflected in the stages of moral development identified by the psychologist, Lawrence Kohlberg[75], represents a developmental view of increasingly differentiated and integrated levels of moral reasoning.

What if a person is *often mistaken about what he believes to be right but he acts from a morally good motive*? Clearly the person's action would not be morally good but the person may not be considered morally bad; he might be considered to be *misguided*. We might say that he means well but he is misguided. The frequency of being mistaken would affect one's judgment about such a person. The degree of wrongness is discussed later.

What about the distinction between *morally good acts* and *morally bad acts*? Is *morally bad* simply the converse of *morally good*? Is an act morally bad because it is wrong and done from a desire to do wrong, just as an act is morally good because it is right and done from a desire to do what is right? Are morally bad acts done from a bad motive ... from a desire to do wrong for the sake of doing wrong?

It is doubtful that people *commit wrong acts because they desire to do wrong for the sake of doing wrong.* For example, a student who is truant from school would seem to be acting from a desire to be absent from school or a desire to be somewhere else and not from a desire to do wrong for wrong's sake. Why would he take the risk of being caught and subsequently punished if there was nothing in it for him? Surely he considered the relative value of what he wants and its consequences when he considered being truant. What might be of interest to him in the desire to do wrong for wrong's sake? It is much more plausible to assume that his object of interest was the desire to be somewhere else or do something else. None of these motives are the same as saying that he was truant from a desire to do wrong for wrong's sake. Ironically, it would seem that when a person does a wrong act, invariably he seems to do it from motives which, in themselves, may not be morally bad.

Do people sometimes *do wrong acts for the sake of doing wrong acts in small matters*? For example, do they get involved in petty theft just for kicks, thereby suggesting that they did what was wrong for wrong's sake? This suggests that they do not pursue an object of interest in doing the wrong act which is a dubious assumption. *Just for kicks* can just as well mean *test the system, for the fun of it,* or *to show that I can do it.* These motives are not analogous to doing something for wrong's sake. In short, it is doubtful that people act from a desire to do wrong for wrong's sake. There is no reason to believe that such a desire is an object of interest for people. Exceptions my include people who suffer from a pathological condition.

Which motives might make a wrong act a morally bad act? It is the absence of a certain sort of motive, namely, the desire to do right (or refrain from doing wrong). In fact, if a person does something which is not wrong but he does it in spite of believing that it is wrong, he is acting immorally. This simply means that he acts in a way in which an immoral person would act. His manner of action reflects a certain property: an indifference to the wrongness of the act. On the other hand, if a person did what was wrong but he believed it to be right and he did it from a desire to do the right thing, he would have acted morally. He would have acted in a way in which a moral person would have acted.

In short, *an act is morally bad* when it is wrong and the perpetrator of the act is not deterred by its wrongness. Motive refers to a person and not an act.

Just as *morally good* can apply to acts so also *morally bad* can apply to people. Who, then, is a morally bad person? *A morally bad person is quite prepared to do a wrong act if it suits his purpose.* It should be noted that he need not actually do the act. In fact, doing a morally wrong act does not necessarily make a person a morally bad person. If a person does a wrong act reluctantly he might be regarded as being a *morally weak* person instead of a morally bad person. The person would be regarded as someone who yielded to temptation. He would be considered a morally weak person if he yields to temptation somewhat frequently or succumbs to temptation in some areas of activity on a regular basis.

On the other hand, *a person who feels no reluctance about doing a wrong act would be regarded as an unscrupulous or unprincipled person.* A thoroughly bad person is regarded as a thoroughly unscrupulous person. He would lack all scruples, which is to say, that he would not be deterred by any sense of wrong. This situation could be brought on by certain *naturally bad motives* such as hatred, revenge, jealousy, envy, greed, lust, or malice. These motives can overcome people when they do not make continuous efforts to deter the influence of naturally bad motives. When these naturally bad motives become strong enough in a person, they can blur the person's sense of right and wrong and so the person can become unscrupulous.

Some people seem to have a *moral blind spot.* They persistently fail to see that what they do in certain areas is wrong. For example, some students tend to get involved in fights from a sense of duty to help an underdog. They apparently fail to see that it is not their duty to engage in fights to help an underdog. There is no reason to believe that they suffer from a pathological condition. They simply have a moral blind spot with regards a certain activity.

Sometimes a person commits such dastardly acts that it is felt that the *person is not in his right mind*. For example, suppose a student thought that it was his duty to hurt his teacher because the teacher made an insulting remark. The student would be regarded as suffering from a pathological condition and therefore his motives would not be viewed as being morally good or bad. He probably would be considered as a person who was not in his right mind.

The levels of moral goodness and moral badness raise the question: *What are the characteristics that make an act good or bad*? Scrupulousness and being principled have already been identified as characteristics which makes an act morally good. Many people claim a third characteristic should be added, namely, *conscience*. It implies that people have a special faculty called a conscience which tells them what is right and wrong and so motivates them to do what is right and deters them from doing what is wrong.

Sometimes the stages of moral goodness and moral badness are not applicable. For example, what about the person who is not indifferent to the wrongness of an act and who desires to do his duty but who is *careless*? This might be viewed as negligent behavior. It is frequently said of such a person that he meant no harm. Should the person act carelessly frequently, his action certainly would not be considered morally good; the person would be regarded as being *irresponsible*. Should he commit some rather seriously wrong act, he would be regarded as being *unscrupulous*.

To illustrate how duty affects motives and moral goodness, I need to draw attention to the use of the word *ought*. The problem is illustrated in the following example:

- John believes that he ought to apologize.
- But in fact it is not the case that he ought to do apologize.
- Ought he then apologize?

This dilemma frequently evokes the following response: *A man ought to do what he believes he ought to do"* or *"since he thought it was the right thing to do, he ought to do it*. At first glance, these responses seem to imply that one's duty is determined by what one thinks to be one's duty. However, this is a case where *ought* is used in two moral senses. In the saying, *A man ought to do what he believes he ought to do*, the term *ought* is used to say that his action would be morally good if he did it and that it would be morally bad if he did not do it. In this case, ought refers to the *motive* of the person. In *What he believes he ought to do*, the term *ought* is used to say that he believes that it would be the right thing for him to do X and it would be the wrong thing for him not to do X. In this case *ought* is used in the moral sense in that it refers to the person's *duty*. Therefore to say *A man ought to do what he believes he ought to do* does not necessarily mean that one's *duty* is determined by what one thinks is one's duty.

Two observations stand out for me. First, it is apparent from the analysis of the word *ought* that some moral terms can be used in more than one sense. Hence, we need to determine the moral sense not only from the choice of moral terms but also from the context in which the terms are used.

Secondly, with each additional class of moral terms and reasoning, a greater variety of moral judgments can be made. Since moral judgments affect the lives of people, it is important that moral judgments be articulated and differentiated as much as possible.

The complex issues surrounding motive are summarized below (Figure 7).

Concepts about Motive	Response
1. What conditions must be fulfilled for an act to be morally good?	The act must be right. The act must be done from a morally good motive.
2. What if a person does an act which is wrong but he believes it to be right and he does it from a morally good motive?	The act is not morally good even though the person would be regarded as a morally good person.
3. What if a person does an act which is right but he does not believe it to be right and his motives are not good?	The person would not be regarded as a morally good person.
4. When is a person driven by a morally good motive?	The person believes that an act is right. The person desires to do what is right.
5. Is *wanting to do one's duty* the same as *wanting to do the right thing*?	Wanting to do one's duty must be distinguished from *wanting to do the right thing*.
6. What do cynics assume is the primary motive?	Cynics assume that people act only from self-interest.
7. Morally good motives must be distinguished from good motives.	Compassion and love are examples of good motives.
8. Moral virtues must be distinguished from non-moral virtues.	Moral virtues reflect a propensity to do what is right from a morally good motive. Non-moral virtues include intellectual virtues like *wit*.
9. Is *morally bad* simply the converse of *morally good*?	No. Morally bad does not refer to the desire to do wrong for the sake of doing wrong.

10. What constitutes a morally bad act?	A morally bad act is done with indifference to do what is right.
11. A morally weak person must be distinguished from a morally bad person.	A morally weak person yields to temptation somewhat frequently but is not considered a morally bad person.
12. What are naturally bad motives?	They include hatred, revenge, jealousy, envy, greed, lust, malice.
13. The range of levels from morally good to moral bad include the following:	- principled reasoning - misguided action - moral blind spot - unscrupulous action
14. What about the person who desires to do his duty but is careless?	- his action is not morally good - he is not a morally bad person
15. The word *ought* includes two moral senses.	- *Ought* can refer to the motive of a person. - *Ought* can refer to a person's duty.

Figure 7: Motive

Young people's view of motive

People who claim that moral choices are just a matter of individual taste do not include morally good motives as a necessary condition for an act to be good. Brooks reminds us that frequently commencement speakers tell graduates "to follow their passion, to trust their feelings, to reflect and find their purpose in life[76]." Young people seem to take that advice to heart.

The young people accept that believing something to be right could be a sufficient motive for doing it. Wanting to do what it is one's duty is not considered a necessary condition. They view *love* as a good motive.

They disregard the distinction between a non-moral person and a moral person. They do not differentiate between morally good motives and naturally good motives. A good motive is a good motive, period. They probably recognize the distinction between the disposition of a person and a person actually doing what is right. They would disregard any reference to people being morally good or virtuous.

According to Brooks, young people regard moral goodness as, "I know I am doing right because I feel harmonious inside. Something is going wrong, on the other hand, when I feel I am not being true to myself[77]." Whether a person is often mistaken or misguided about what he believes to be right would be immaterial to them. As Brooks points out, young people maintain that "You know you are doing the right thing when you feel good inside. The valid rules of life are those you make or accept for yourself and that feel right for you[78]." They probably agree that people, who commit wrong acts, do so with indifference as to the wrongness of the action and not because they desire to do wrong for the sake of doing wrong. Nor would people commit wrong acts for wrong's sake in small matters such as getting involved in petty thefts just for kicks.

Brooks reports that young people place "great emphasis ... on personal feelings as a guide for what is right and wrong[79]." He maintains this is the motive driving young people today. They probably would agree that a bad person is someone who is prepared to do wrong; they are motivated by naturally bad motives such as anger. They agree that there are some degrees of badness only to the extent that rape and murder are considered wrong. However, Brooks points out that aside from agreeing on these two extreme cases, "moral thinking didn't enter the picture for them, even when considering issues like drunk driving, cheating in school or cheating on a partner[80]."

They would not acknowledge moral blind spots. For them there is no such thing as persistently failing to see that certain acts are wrong except for rape and murder. They would not judge a person they thought was not in his right mind. They might agree that people have a special faculty called a conscience only if *conscience* refers to individual preferences.

According to Brooks, young people seem to acknowledge that they can improve themselves: "you have to be taught to love yourself, to be true to yourself ...[81]." This observation by Brooks, I would argue, is the most redeeming aspect of his account of young people. However, it leaves Brooks with the following challenge: How would he teach young people to make the transition from *loving yourself* to developing the emotional motive of empathy? We will see in the following conversation between Bill and Mae the significance of having a sense of empathy.

Conversation about motive - Bill and Mae

Let's return to Bill and Mae's conversation. This time they focus on motives beginning with the motive that prompted Bill's feeling of disappointment.

"TGIF!" exclaimed Bill who had had a disappointing week. The State Math Test results had just been released and his class had not improved as much as the State required. Consequently, he had not received the State Teacher of the Month Award and $10,000.00 for learning supplies for his school. He had tried so hard and his students had improved a lot on the State Math Exam. Yet he felt he had failed.

When Mae and Bill met as usual during the noon lunch break, Mae immediately observed Bill's disappointment. She was not quite sure about the reason for his disappointment. Bill's students had improved their performance significantly and the principal had congratulated Bill for his stellar effort, especially with the disadvantaged children in his class. So why was Bill so dejected? Mae wondered whether Bill's driving motive really had been about receiving the Teacher of the Month Award and not only about the performance of his students. If it was about the former, Mae would be disappointed in Bill. As a friend, she felt she should raise this sensitive issue. But, how? Certainly, she could not confront him about his motive. He might accuse her of imputing a motive. Maybe, they could explore the concept of motives together and see what happens.

Mae started their conversation about motives with a question that has been raised a number of times before, "Suppose Peter helped a blind man cross the street so that the blind man would not have an accident. Was his motive morally good?" Before Bill could answer, she gave the obvious answer, "The reason given for helping the blind man reflects a morally good motive." That led to the question Mae really wanted to ask, "What if Peter does an act which is actually wrong but he believes it to be right and he does it from a morally good motive?"

Bill took the bait by responding, "It would not be a morally good act if the action itself is wrong because one of the conditions of a morally good act would not have been satisfied."

"Does that make Peter a morally bad person?" asked Mae.

"Your question seems to confuse morally bad act with morally bad person," accused Bill. "A person can be mistaken about what he believes and consequently commit a morally bad act. That does not necessarily make him a morally bad person."

Mae continued by posing this question, "Is an act morally good when a person does an act which is right but he does not believe it to be right? Suppose a principal did the right thing by requiring a student to repeat a grade due to failing grades, but he did not believe it was the right thing to do. Would his act be morally good?"

Bill didn't think so. He maintained, "For the principal's act to be morally good, it must be right and done from a morally good motive. His motive was not morally good because he did what he thought was the wrong thing to do."

Mae offered another situation, "Suppose the Principal is motivated to fail a student with poor grades because the student is a trouble maker in school. His action for failing the student would not be based on a morally good motive, namely, a desire to do what is right but would be based on a decision to punish the student for being a troublemaker. I maintain his action would not be morally good."

Mae pointed out an important distinction about motives, "Wanting to do one's duty must be distinguished from wanting to do the right thing. Suppose," she said, "John, another teacher at her school, simply wanted to do his duty of playground supervision during the afternoon recess at his elementary school. He paid no attention to how the children played together nor how they excluded a new child at their school. He would not have met the condition of wanting to do the right thing."

Bill had to agree with her. He wondered how his friend, Jim, who is a cynic, might respond to the issue of acting from a morally good motive. So he asked, "How might a cynic respond?"

Mae was quick to respond, "The cynic does not believe that people act from morally good motives but act purely from self-interest. For example, when a teacher stays after school to help a student with his math, the cynic would maintain that the teacher does it from an ulterior motive of self-interest and not from a desire to do what is right. He probably wants to make sure that his class does well on the school-wide math exam to show his principal what a good teacher he is. It's called protecting your job."

Mae reminded Bill, "There are other good motives besides the desire to do what is right or to do one's duty. For example, compassion and love are considered good motives but I don't think they are morally good motives."

She went on in great detail explaining why love is not a morally good motive, even though many people probably would assume that acting out of love is acting from a morally good motive. For example, she said, "Suppose a parent helps her daughter with her homework day after day out of love. She would be acting from a good motive, *love*, but not necessarily from a morally good motive."

Bill interjected, "Nor are all virtues *moral virtues*. For example, wit, quickness of thought, is regarded as an *intellectual virtue*, not a moral virtue."

"But," added Mae, "Some virtues, like *truthfulness*, are regarded as moral virtues. They are regarded as moral virtues because telling the truth is the right thing to do. They reflect a disposition to do what is the right thing to do. In other words, a moral virtue is a disposition to do what is right from a morally good motive."

Bill asked, "Is a virtuous person the same as a morally good person?"

Mae observed, "This question distinguishes a person who is actually doing something from someone with a disposition to act. *Morally good* refers to the disposition of a person to tell the truth, be friendly, or be generous which are morally good motives. *Virtuous*, on the other hand, refers to a person who is actually doing what is right. A virtuous person resists, with persistence, the temptation to do wrong acts such as degrading other people, committing odious or dastardly deeds, or living a degenerate life."

This distinction made Mae think about Bill's disappointment about not receiving the State Teacher of the Month Award. No doubt, Bill is a morally good person. But, was Bill acting like a virtuous person? She was not certain; she was not going to raise this question.

Bill interrupted Mae's thoughts by asking, "What if a person is often *mistaken* about what he believes to be right but he acts from a morally good motive?"

Quickly recovering from her reflections about Bill, Mae responded, "The person would not be considered morally bad; he might be considered to be *misguided*. People might say that he means well but he is misguided."

Bill raised a question which, he thought had an obvious answer, "Is *morally bad* simply the converse of *morally good*? In other words, is a person morally bad because he acted from a desire to do wrong just like a person is morally good because he acted from a desire to do what is right?" More to the point Bill rephrased his question, "Do people commit bad acts sometimes for the sake of doing wrong?" Quietly to himself, Bill felt the obvious answer is *yes*.

Mae was not so sure. This is how she put it, "I doubt that people commit wrong acts because they desire to do wrong for the sake of doing wrong."

Bill interjected, "Of course people sometimes engage in wrong acts for the sake of doing wrong. I see it all the time! Remember the time when one of my students went fishing without telling his parents or the school? I'll bet he did it just to prove that he could stay away from school. He never goes fishing on his own!"

Patiently, Mae responded with an example to support her view, "A student who is truant would seem to be acting from a desire to be absent from school or a desire to be somewhere else and not from a desire to do wrong for wrong's sake. Why would he take the risk of being caught and be punished if there was nothing in it for him? Surely he considered the implications of being truant. What would be of interest to him in the desire to do wrong for wrong's sake? It is much more likely that he desired to be somewhere else or do something else. None of these motives are the same as saying that he was truant from a desire to do wrong for wrong's sake."

She added, "Ironically, it would seem that when a person does a wrong act, invariably he seems to do it from motives which, in themselves, may not be morally bad. You mentioned one of your students went fishing when he should have been at school. There is nothing wrong with his motive to go fishing per se even though it was wrong for him to be truant."

In defence of his view, Bill maintained, "People sometimes do wrong for the sake of doing wrong in small matters. They get involved in petty theft just for kicks. This suggests to me that sometimes people do wrong for wrong's sake."

Mae countered, "Once again, I don't see why people would do wrong for the sake of doing wrong. *Just for kicks* can just as well mean *test the system* or *for the fun of it* or *to show that one can do it*. These motives are not the same as doing wrong for wrong's sake." She summed it up by saying, "It is doubtful that people act from a desire to do wrong for wrong's sake. There is no reason to believe that such a desire is of interest to anyone. Only people suffering from a pathological condition might desire to do wrong for wrong's sake."

Bill was still troubled with the notion of bad motives. So he asked, "What could be a bad motive which makes a wrong act a morally bad act?"

'I think,' Mae maintained, "bad motive refers to an absence of a desire to do right or refrain from doing wrong."

Bill retorted, "Are you saying that, if a person does something which is not wrong but he does it in spite of believing that it is wrong, he might feel he is acting immorally? Suppose one of my students, Jerry, believes it is wrong for him to ask his mother for help with a difficult math homework assignment. Since Jerry believes that the teacher expects him to do the math assignment without help, he might feel guilty even though it was not wrong for his mother to help him. She had every right to support her son when he was struggling with his homework assignment."

"Yes," replied Mae. "That simply means that he acted in a way in which an immoral person would act, act with indifference to the wrongness of an act."

Once again Bill asked, "What if a person did what was wrong but he believed it to be right and he did it from a desire to do the right thing, Would he have acted morally?"

"I'm afraid so," replied Mae. "He would have acted in a way in which a moral person acts."

Bill was not convinced.

Mae made one more attempt at clarifying what she meant by morally bad acts, "An act is morally bad when it is wrong and a person does not care whether it is wrong. When an act is very bad, morally, it is judged to be evil, atrocious, wicked, fiendish, or demonic." She added, "What makes an act morally worse is the degree of the seriousness of the wrong act. For example, it is more seriously wrong to murder a person than to steal a car."

Frustrated, Bill fired back, "Who, then, is a morally bad person?"

Patiently, Mae explained, "A morally bad person is quite prepared to do a morally wrong act if it suits his purpose. He does not care whether the act is right or wrong"

Then she cautioned, "A person need not actually do the act. In fact, doing a morally wrong act does not necessarily make a person a morally bad person."

"Should all morally bad acts be treated equally?" asked Bill.

To which Mae responded, "Of course not! If a person does a wrong act reluctantly he might be regarded a morally weak person instead of a morally bad person. The act would be regarded as yielding to temptation. On the other hand, a person, who feels no reluctance about doing a wrong act, would be regarded as an unscrupulous person. He would lack all scruples, which is to say, he would not be deterred by any sense of wrong. Morally bad acts should not be treated equally."

"So who would be so unscrupulous?" asked Bill.

"It might be a person who is motivated by certain naturally bad motives like hatred, revenge, jealousy, envy, greed, lust, or malice," replied Mae. "These are motives which can overcome people when they do not make continuous efforts to deter the influence of naturally bad motives. When these naturally bad motives become strong enough in a person, they can blur the person's sense of right and wrong to the point where the person can become unscrupulous."

Mae was concerned that Bill might view her in black and white terms about motives. So she made a few more distinctions, "Some people seem to have a moral blind spot. They persistently fail to see that what they do is wrong. For example, a student may get involved in fights to help an underdog from a sense of duty. He apparently fails to see that it is not his duty to engage in fights to help an underdog. There is no reason to believe that he suffers from a pathological condition. He simply may have a moral blind spot with regard to fighting for an underdog."

Bill pointed out, "Sometimes we say a person, who committed a dastardly act, is not in his right mind. What's that person's motive?"

"Excuse me for using a dramatic example to answer your question," replied Mae. "Suppose a student thought it was his duty to hurt his teacher because the teacher made an insulting remark about him. The student could be regarded as suffering from a pathological condition and therefore his motives would not be viewed in terms of moral goodness or moral badness. He probably would be considered as a person who was not in his right mind."

"Where does a person's conscience fit into the picture?" asked Bill.

Mae felt she was not on secure ground in responding to this question ... she had had questions about what constitutes a conscience for many years; so she expressed her own belief, "I believe people have a special faculty called a conscience which sometimes tells them what is right and wrong. It can motivate people to do what is right and deter them from doing what is wrong. But," she added," I think there is more to it than that but I am not sure what it is."

Mae's responses drove Bill to ask more questions; he was convinced there had to be a flaw in Mae's view of motives. The notion of motives was too elusive a concept to be subject to her definitive answers. So he asked, "What about the person who is not indifferent to the wrongness of an act and who desires to do his duty but who is careless?"

Mae's responses were becoming less definitive when she replied, "This person's action might be viewed as negligent behavior. It is frequently said of such a person that he meant no harm."

This had been a difficult conversation. Why? With each additional class of moral terms and judgments, a greater variety of moral thinking applies.

The conversation never picked up on Bill's motive for being despondent for not receiving the State Teacher of the Month Award. Suddenly just as they were ready to return to their classes, Bill made what appeared to be an offhand comment about his feeling of disappointment. He muttered to himself, "My motive was miss-directed; I should have kept my focus on the success of my students. They did not let me down; they demonstrated outstanding performance. I let myself down."

Mae was pleasantly surprised and extremely pleased at Bill's candor. At the same time, she had been perturbed ever since their earlier discussion about compassion and love. She felt Bill had implied that somehow the reference to compassion as a 'good motive' and not a 'morally good motive' degraded the importance of compassion and love. She had to take issue with this assumption.

Out of nowhere, Mae added, "I think that morally good motives and empathy go together! It's ridiculous to separate them. In fact, what could possibly drive a person to action more than the emotional energy of empathy?" Before Bill could respond, Mae continued, "What is more likely to drive a young person to assist an older person to cross a busy street safely? Would it be a cold calculated assessment of the likelihood that the older person might get hit by a car as he stumbles across the street? Or, might the young person feel a sense of concern or empathy for the older person while the young person considers the risk of allowing the older person cross the street by himself? In fact, I am convinced that empathy is needed for people to act from morally good motives."

"WOW," Bill muttered. "I never thought of it that way. Maybe we need to consider both. Thanks, Mae."

This had indeed been a EUEKA MOMENT for both of them. Would it change their conversation from here on out? Only time will tell.

A week later ...

It took a week before Bill and Mae could share a lunch hour again. Mae was ready with her question; she was curious about the motives that drive young people according to Brooks. So she asked, "How do young people view morally good motives?"

Bill was surprised that Mae would ask this question. He countered, "Why are you asking? Why would they bother with morally good motives when doing one's duty and having rights are purely personal? Obviously, any motive they might have would be fine! They would assume," he continued "believing something to be right would be a sufficient motive for doing it."

"Are you saying that wanting to do what is right from a morally good motive is immaterial to them?" asked Mae.

"I believe so," replied Bill. "They see motives simply as a personal state of mind."

"Would they regard love as a good motive?" asked Mae.

"Probably," Bill explained, "I don't think they differentiate between morally good motives and naturally good motives. A good motive is a good motive, period!"

"It follows it seems to me," Mae continued, "that there is no hierarchy of moral goodness. Nor can people be mistaken or misguided about what they believe to be right because you know you are doing the right thing when you feel good inside."

To which Bill added, "They do not consider acting with indifference or a desire to do wrong for wrong's sake as wrong acts."

Mae reiterated, "They place great emphasis on personal feelings as a guide for what is right and wrong. This seems to be the motive driving young people."

"Is there such a thing as naturally bad motives as they see it?" wondered Bill.

"Possibly," responded Mae. "Naturally bad motives might drive some people to commit rape and murder which they agree are wrong."

Bill could not resist asking an impossible question, "Do they believe that people have a special faculty called a conscience?"

"They probably do not believe that people have a conscience which tells them what is right and wrong," replied Mae. Not to be outdone, she asked, "Do they accept that sometimes people are careless?"

Bill countered by asking, "How can people be careless when moral choices are just a matter of individual taste?"

Mae did not respond because the answer to that question seemed obvious to her.

Once again, it was time for Mae and Bill to return to their classes. They were determined to pick up on their conversation at the next opportunity.

We have now seen how Bill and Mae understand the first three categories of the Principled Thinking Model: *duties, rights* and *motive*. Let's see what is meant by the category, *desert*, and how Bill and Mae view it. *Desert* refers to what people deserve as a result of their action, both morally good and bad action.

Chapter 8
Desert

Conceptual Framework[82]

We often talk about what a person deserves. Look at this brief story about David Suzuki.

> David Suzuki is a well-known biologist and outspoken environmentalist who was born on March 24, 1936, the eldest son of the Suzuki family. His interest in public speaking developed when he was in Junior High School. He went on to win public speaking contests, often speaking about conserving nature. After working in several universities, Suzuki moved to the University of British Columbia where he continued his research in biology. Today, Suzuki shares his environmental concerns with the world through his TV program, *The Nature of Things*[83]

We might be inclined to recommend that Suzuki deserves a public commendation, possibly an honorary degree in Philosophy, for his contribution to making people aware of the need to conserve nature.

On the other hand, look at this story about Thierry Henry.

> The French captain, Thierry Henry, has become the subject of international outrage as many from Irish fans and their Prime Minister to French gym teachers condemn the captain's decision not to admit to handling

the ball in the build-up to a goal that eliminated Ireland and sent his team to the World Cup finals.

David McCarthy, an Alberta provincial team soccer coach, has seen 12-year-olds admit to bad plays that referees have missed. But a video showing French Captain Thierry Henry remaining silent about the handling of a ball that led to the game-tying goal has Mr. McCarthy worried. Will he witness less honour among young players on community soccer fields in the future? "What action should have been taken about Captain Henry's conduct?" McCarthy wondered.

Many people insisted that Captain Henry deserved a strong form of disapproval, maybe even some form of punishment. They condemned his decision not to admit to handling the ball.[84]

These two stories highlight the concern and importance placed on what people deserve, also known as desert.

I raise questions and issues about desert in this Chapter. Here are a few:
- Approvals are not wilful. They are psychological states of being.
- A person deserves disapproval for willingly doing a wrong act.
- What if a person planned to commit a wrong act but failed to execute it? What does he deserve?
- Does a person deserve punishment for willing to do wrong?

For a complete list of the questions and statements discussed on *desert*, go to Figure 8 in this Chapter.

Key words

This class of terms and judgments is made up of the representative term, *deserve*, plus at least two more terms, *worthy* and *merit*. *Deserve* is used most commonly. For example, "He deserves to be punished" refers to the act of inflicting an object of disinterest or pain on a person. *Worthy* is used mainly with reference to motives. For example, "Ms Jones was worthy of the Math Teacher Award because she worked successfully with all her math students." Her motive was to see every child in her class succeed in math. *Merit* is used to refer to the quality of the action as well as the actor. For example, "Ms. Jones merited the Award because of her success and her commitment to help all students."

Although I focus on the use of terms in the *moral sense*, deserve is also frequently used in a *non-moral sense*. The non-moral sense is used in this sentence: "The teacher deserves the attention of the class." The moral sense is used in this sentence: "The boy who stole the lunch deserves to be punished."

Moral judgments are not only made about the act, the actor and the interrelationship of the two; but also about the *consequences of moral or immoral acts.* Take for example, "He did not deserve the reward because he cheated on his exam." The consequence of cheating was that he did not deserve the award.

Judgments about whether a person deserves something usually take the following form:

Z (moral person) deserves X on account of Y

Z - is the logical subject even though it is not always the grammatical subject. In the sentence, "Bob deserves punishment for hitting John with a stick", Bob is the logical and grammatical subject.

X - is an object of interest or disinterest. In the example cited above, X is an object of disinterest, namely, punishment. When X is an object of disinterest, it means that Z deserves an expression of disapproval or punishment. When 'X' is an object of interest, it means that Z deserves an expression of approval or a reward.

Y - provides the reasons for stating that Z deserves an object of interest or disinterest.

In the sentence, "Bob deserves punishment for hitting John with a stick," Bob deserves punishment because of his action, namely, for hitting John with a stick. When a person claims that a certain person deserves punishment or a reward but does not offer a reason for the judgment, people usually retort by asking, *Why?* This typical response suggests that a person is expected to offer reasons, implicitly or explicitly, for making the claim that someone deserves punishment or a reward.

Key ideas

People frequently take issue with the *reasons* offered. For example, Bob's friend, Jack, might disagree with the reasons offered by their teacher for insisting that Bob deserves a particular punishment. Tom might disagree with the teacher as to whether Bob deserves any punishment at all. Bill might agree with the teacher that Bob deserves punishment but might maintain that the punishment should be different (i.e., less or more severe). In short, Y is an important aspect of determining whether Z deserves punishment or a reward and what form it should take.

When the teacher says that Bob deserves something, the teacher means that Bob deserves either an object of interest or an object of disinterest. *Objects of disinterest* take one of two forms - *disapproval* or *punishment*. Disapproval is a mild form which is frequently expressed in the form of a frown, words of disappointment, mild censure, or mild criticism. Although an attitude of disapproval is not something one has wilfully, often a person can choose what form the feeling of disapproval should take. When disapproval is expressed in a stronger form, it is usually referred to as punishment. Punishment includes an attitude of disapproval but a feeling of disapproval does not necessarily include punishment.

Objects of interest can also take one of two forms – approval or reward. Mild forms of approval include a nod, words of praise, or a pat on the back. Mild forms of approval are commonly expressed to a person who has done his duty. When approval is expressed in stronger terms, it is usually referred to as a reward, which includes an approval, but takes on a more substantial form such as a gift. Rewards are usually reserved for two kinds of situations. A person may deserve a reward when she has completed a difficult task which many people may not even try or which they frequently fail to complete. For example, a young person might receive a reward for rescuing a drowning child. Second, a person is frequently rewarded for doing something which is beyond the call of duty. For example, a physical education teacher may reward a student for staying after school regularly to clean up the gym equipment. Keeping up this kind of schedule voluntarily, many people might consider going beyond the call of duty.

I need to mention an important distinction between *approval* and *reward*. Awards can be given or withheld at will but approvals are not wilful. An attitude of approval is a psychological state; one either has it or does not have it. A person may choose to try to hide it so that other people will not detect it or choose to give expression to it through words of praise or some other form.

Sometimes it is said that *a thing can also take a punishment*. For example, Tom might say "The boat took a real punishment in the turbulent waters". When he claims that the boat took a real punishment, he is not suggesting that the boat deserved the beating from the waves. It is just a way of talking about the treatment the boat underwent. This example of the use of the term *punishment* does not include a moral sense.

That leads me to the question, "*On account of what actions judged morally, does a person deserve approval?*" As was pointed out earlier, a person probably deserves some form of approval for doing his duty from a sense of duty or for doing what is right for right's sake. People deserve approval for having done morally good acts, acting from morally good motives, and deliberately refraining from doing wrong acts.

Ordinarily, *a person does not deserve a reward* for *having done a morally good act*, that is, for an act which is right and was done from a morally good motive or from a desire to do one's duty. A person does not deserve a reward for acting from a morally good motive alone. For example, a teacher whose motive is to help all children in class succeed in their studies does not deserve a reward. Her morally good motive is not enough; she must also do a morally good act. A person does not deserve a reward for deliberately not doing something which is wrong. For example, a student does not deserve a reward for not teasing a new student in her class. A person does not deserve a reward for being a morally good person, that is, a person who has a disposition to do what is right. For example, a student who is considerate towards fellow students could be considered a morally good person, but he would not deserve a reward for his disposition towards others in class.

In short, people *deserve rewards* only for the two kinds of actions mentioned earlier, namely, when a person performs a difficult task which many people frequently fail to perform or when a person does something which is beyond the call of duty. In most situations people do not deserve anything more than approval. An attitude of approval is a psychological state; one either has it or does not have it. A person may choose to try to hide it or give expression to it through words of praise. People display their approval in different ways: a nod, slap on the back, or a word of approval.

A person *deserves disapproval or an informal expression of disapproval* for the following actions. A person deserves disapproval for being willing to do a wrong act. This should not be confused with maintaining that people do wrong for wrong's sake. Second, a person deserves disapproval for doing a morally wrong act. Third, a person deserves disapproval if he is a morally bad person, that is, a person who is indifferent to the wrongness of his act. A morally bad person might do what is right but doesn't; instead he engages in wrong acts whenever it suits him.

A *person deserves punishment* for the following action. A person deserves punishment for committing a seriously wrong act with indifference as its wrongness. For example, a person who snatches a purse from a woman should be punished because the purse-snatcher has committed a wrong act with indifference as to its wrongness.

A person *does not deserve the same degree of punishment* for any and all morally bad acts. The magnitude of the punishment inflicted upon a person should be in proportion to the seriousness of the wrong act committed. The more seriously wrong an act is, the more severe the punishment should be. Take, for example, the issue of *life vs. property*. Since it is more seriously wrong to take the life of a person than destroying property, the former is considered a more serious crime and therefore should be punished more seriously.

A person may not deserve punishment for *willing to do wrong but not doing it*. As a rule, such a person would only deserve an expression of disapproval. Suppose in a fit of anger, a teenager threatened to challenge a classmate to a fight on the way home from school, but did not follow through with the challenge for a fight. In the morning after, the vice principal of his school, who had been tipped off about the potential fight, called the teenage to the office. When the vice principal was informed that the fight never took place, she cautioned the teenage not to make these kinds of threats because they make students and staff anxious about their safety at school.

If a person *planned to commit a wrong act, such as robbing a bank, tried to execute it, but failed to do it*, the person deserves to be punished. The person deserves some form of punishment because he acted in a manner designed to inflict harm on other people. For example, conspiracy is not just a matter of being willing to do wrong; it is an act of planning and organizing steps to inflict harm on other people. Planning and organizing deliberate harm is part of the process of executing the harmful act and therefore deserves some form of punishment.

Does a person deserve *punishment for sins of omission* such as failure to do one's duty? Possibly, for it is wrong not to do one's duty. Of course, it would have to be established clearly that the person had a duty to do the act in question. In some instances, that is easy. For example, if John has a duty to deliver a message, it probably can be established whether or not he did it. In other situations it is much more difficult to determine one's duty. For example, what is the duty of a working single parent who is unable to get her son to school on time? It is frequently very difficult to determine sins of omission. At the same time, that does not make the question concerning sins of omission irrelevant.

There appears to be a direct connection between *desert* and *motive*. I have said in different ways that a person deserves approval or rewards for wanting to do what is the right thing to do and disapproval or punishment for being indifferent about doing the right thing. In other words, judgments about *desert* take into account the *motive* of the person as well as the act itself.

For example, suppose a teacher has to decide whether a young boy deserves punishment for throwing a snowball across the street and hitting a passing car. The teacher must consider whether throwing snowballs is wrong when it accidentally hits a moving vehicle. The wrongness of the act could be established by checking with the Highway Traffic Act or by considering the possible consequences of startling a driver. The teacher should also consider the boy's motives. Did the boy intend to throw the snowball at the car or was he throwing it at a friend, or an object located across the street? If it could be established that the boy intended to hit the moving vehicle, his motive would have been bad. In that case, since the act in question was wrong and done from a morally wrong motive, the boy committed a morally bad act. The teacher must decide whether the boy deserves to be punished or whether he should get an expression of disapproval. This involves making a judgment about what the boy deserves and the seriousness of the act which is by no means easy. People frequently disagree on the seriousness of the wrong act and subsequently on what form of disapproval or punishment a person deserves.

The implications of this disagreement can be quite significant. For example, teachers may have different viewpoints about the seriousness of throwing snowballs and hitting moving cars. Some might consider it from the possibility of causing the driver to lose control of the vehicle and consequently getting involved in an accident. A teacher with this viewpoint would consider the act as being seriously wrong and therefore the teacher might insist that the boy deserves a more serious form of punishment. Another teacher might view the snowball throwing as little more than an annoying incident to a driver. The wrong act would not be considered as seriously wrong by this teacher and therefore a milder form of punishment probably would be considered appropriate.

That the question of *desert* is taken very seriously by people of all ages, is evidenced by the fact that people have strong feelings about awards and punishment. This is apparent in the day to day interaction at home, in school, in the community, at work, in the legislature, and the courts. As I have indicated above, school administrators and teachers must frequently make discretionary decisions about what punishment or reward a student deserves.

Desert, what people deserve, is a fundamental part of resolving moral dilemmas as is shown in the following chart (Figure 8).

Concepts about Desert	Responses
1. Standard form for desert: Z deserves X on account of Y.	Z is the moral agent X is an object of interest or disinterest Y provides the reasons for allocating an object of interest or inflicting an object of disinterest
2. Objects of disinterest deserve:	- disapproval or punishment
3. Objects of interest deserve:	- approval or reward
4. Awards	- can be given or withheld at will
5. Approvals and disapprovals	- are psychological states of being that are not wilful
6. Acts of disapproval include the following:	- a frown, words of disappointment, mild censure, or mild criticism

7. Acts of approval include the following:	- a smile, words of praise, a nod, slap on the back
8. For what does a person deserve approval?	- doing one's duty or doing a morally good act from a morally good motive
9. For what does a person deserve a reward?	- performing a difficult task or - going beyond the call of duty – called an act of supererogation
10. Normally, a person is not rewarded for:	- morally good action - morally good motive - not doing something that is wrong - being a moral agent - doing one's duty
11. A person deserves disap-proval for:	- willingly doing a wrong act - being a morally bad person
12. On account of what does a person deserve punishment?	- committing a morally wrong act with indiffer-ence as to the wrongness of the act
13. Do all bad acts deserve the same degree of punishment?	- The punishment should be in proportion to the seriousness of the wrong act
14. Does a person deserve pun-ishment for willing to do wrong?	- deserves some form of disapproval
15. What if a person planned to commit a wrong act but failed to execute it?	- deserves some form of punishment
16. Does a person deserve punishment for failure to do his duty?	- possibly, though sometimes an expression of disapproval may be appropriate

Figure 8: Desert

Young people's view of desert

The young people according to Brooks do not seem to distinguish the moral sense of the term *desert* from the non-moral sense. When they were asked by a research team "to identify a moral dilemma they had faced, two-thirds of the young people either couldn't answer the question or [shifted to describing] problems that are not moral at all[85]." For example, when they were asked to describe a moral dilemma, they couldn't think of one; they talked about being able to afford the rent on an apartment or whether they had enough quarters to feed a parking meter. These issues reflect a non-moral sense.

I should emphasize that Brooks, does not agree with the position taken by the young people involved in the study conducted by Christian Smith. Brooks makes his position clear in *The Road to Character*[86] published in 2015.

It is not certain that the young people would expect a person to offer reasons, implicitly or explicitly, for making the claim that someone deserves some form of punishment or reward. If moral choices are just a matter of individual taste, why offer any reasons? Individual taste is reason enough, so they seem to claim. For example, they did not consider cheating on tests at school a moral issue. That is to say, cheating at school is neither right nor wrong. It's up to each individual whether to cheat or not to cheat. You don't have to offer any reasons for your personal choice.

Brooks suggests that, for young people, the ultimate reward is achieving self-determination: "If you define a realistic purpose early on and execute your strategy flexibly, you will wind up leading a purposeful life. You will have achieved self-determination[87]."

The young people would concur with the position taken in this book that approvals or disapproval are not wilful but reflect a psychological state of mind. A person may be able to choose what form the feeling of approval or disapproval might take. Brooks observes that young people tend to organize their lives on the basis of "a method that begins with the self and ends with the self; begins with self-investigation and ends with self-fulfillment[88]." He maintains that the young people have rejected blind deference to authority and have shifted to other forms of what makes them happy.

No doubt, they would agree that sometimes people punish someone out of frustration. However, they show little interest in any form of punishment or reward. A person does not deserve a reward in most situations. According to Brooks, "[They] go through life as a self-contained unit, coolly weighing risks and rewards and looking out for [their] own interests[89]" The only bad acts acknowledged by the young people in the study reviewed by Brooks are crimes of rape or murder. For these two crimes, a person probably deserves some form of punishment for acting with indifference as to the wrongness of the acts.

Brooks reports that young people pay little attention to what people deserve because they focus on the self as indicated in the following statement: "We tend to prize the freedom to navigate as we wish, to run our lives as we choose, and never to submerge our own individual identities in conformity to some bureaucracy or organization[90]." They probably feel that people do not deserve punishment for planning but failing to commit a wrong act. Nor would they approve of any form of punishment for committing sins of omission. As has been mentioned, they take the question of desert seriously only as it relates to rape and murder. Even when considering things like "drunken driving, cheating in school or cheating on a partner, moral thinking didn't enter the picture[91]" for them according to the Study reviewed by Brooks.

In summary, Brooks suggests that the young people show little interest in what people deserve. Their focus is best described as follows, "We tend to believe that the 'true self' is whatever is most natural or untutored. That is, each of us has a certain sincere way of being in the world, and we should live our life being truthful to that authentic inner self, not succumbing to the pressure outside ourselves[92]."

I agree with Brooks that the young people in the study by Christian Smith seem to have shifted to a subjective view of moral dilemmas by viewing them as personal concerns and interests.

Conversation about desert - Bill and Mae

The conversation between Mae and Bill reflects their various experiences as teachers and the books they have read. This time it was triggered by what Mae was reading. As part of the reading requirements for her final course towards her M. Ed., she was reading *The Better Angels of our Nature* by Steve Pinker. She was struck by what Pinker said about *just desert*: "The rationale for criminal justice ... also embraces just deserts which is basically a citizen's impulse for revenge[93]."

"Revenge?" thought Mae. "How can *just desert* be revenge?" She was uneasy about Pinker's explanation of just desert; so she read this quote from Pinker to Bill: "Criminal punishment is often harsher than what would be needed as a finely tuned incentive designed to minimize the society's sum of harm ... Even if we were certain that the perpetrator of a heinous crime would never offend again nor set an example for anyone else, most people would feel that *justice must be done* and that he should incur some harm to balance the harm he caused[94]."

Mae was about to frame the argument for what and why a moral person deserves something when Bill interrupted her to point out, "Desert can be and frequently is used in a non-moral sense as well." He gave an obvious example, "A teacher deserves the attention of the class." At the same time, he acknowledged, "Deserve is used commonly in the moral sense as in, 'The boy who stole the lunch deserves to be punished.'"

Mae agreed and returned to her view of desert, "A person deserves something for specific reasons. Take this example," she said, "Jim deserves some form of punishment because he broke Betty's bicycle. In this case Jim deserves some form of punishment for a specific reason, namely, he broke Betty's bicycle!"

"Why is it so difficult to determine what people deserve?" asked Bill.

Mae could think of a few as she recalled her friends' argument about what form of punishment Jim deserved for cheating on a recent history exam. She listed a few: "John disagreed with Betty by maintaining that Jim does not deserve any punishment at all. Kelly disagreed with the reasons offered by Betty for claiming that Jim deserved to be punished. James agreed with Betty that Jim deserved punishment but maintained that the punishment should be more severe. So, there can be lots of reasons why people might disagree on what people deserve."

Bill observed, "I guess the same applies to deserving approval. Giving reasons is obviously very important."

To which Mae added, "When approval is expressed in stronger terms, it is usually referred to as a reward, which includes an approval, but adds a more substantial form such as a gift."

"Rewards are usually reserved for special occasions," Bill noted. "A person may deserve a reward when she has completed a difficult task which many people may not even try or which they frequently fail to complete. For example, a young person might deserve a reward for rescuing a drowning child."

Mae thought of another situation, "A person is frequently rewarded for doing something which is beyond the call of duty. For example, a teacher might offer to do lunch duty for a colleague recovering from an illness. In response, the principal may reduce the volunteer's lunch duty."

To sum up the difference between approval and reward, Bill concluded, "Awards can be given or withheld at will but approvals are not wilful. An attitude of approval is a psychological state: one either has it or does not have it. A person may choose to try to hide it or give expression to it through words of praise."

Shifting to objects of disinterest, Mae pointed out, "Objects of disinterest also take two forms: disapproval and punishment. A teacher might express her disapproval of a student's remark in class in the form of a frown."

Again, Bill interjected, "Although an attitude of disapproval is not something one has wilfully, often a person can choose how to express it."

Mae continued, "When disapproval is expressed in a stronger form, we refer to it as punishment which, by the way, includes a feeling of disapproval."

"But expressing disapproval does not necessarily include punishment," added Bill. He went on to ask, "For what ought a person be punished?" Since Mae hesitated to respond to the question, Bill continued, "Probably, a person should be punished for doing a wrong act with indifference as to its wrongness."

Mae agreed.

As an aside, Bill recalled a non-moral use of the word punishment. "Our truck took a real punishment on the washboard gravel road to the remote ancient fishing village. Of course the truck did not deserve the beating. It was just a way of talking about the damage to our truck."

Although Mae did not like to focus on disapproval, she stated, "A person deserves disapproval for willingly doing a wrong act." She was quick to add, "This should not be confused with saying that sometimes people do wrong for wrong's sake."

"Do people deserve the same degree of punishment for any and all morally bad acts?" asked Bill.

"The more seriously wrong an act is, the more severe the punishment should be," responded Mae.

"Does a person deserve punishment for being willing to do wrong but not do it?" asked Bill.

"That sounds like a silly question, responded Mae. "Who would do that?"

'I don't know," replied Bill, "but probably the person would only deserve an expression of disapproval."

Mae added a clarification by pointing out, "Conspiracy is not just a matter of being willing to do wrong; it is an act of planning and organizing steps to inflict harm on other people." Then Mae added another twist to the issue of what people deserve by asking, "What if a person planned to commit a wrong act, such as robbing a bank, tried to execute it, but failed to do it? Does he deserve to be punished?"

Bill asserted, "The person would deserve some form of punishment, because he acted in a manner designed to inflict harm on other people."

Mae added yet another twist by asking, "Does a person deserve punishment for sins of omission such as failure to do one's chores at home?"

This question requires an explanation about duty thought Bill. So he responded by saying, "Possibly, because it is wrong not to do one's duty. In many instances, it is easy to determine someone's duty. For example, if John has a duty to deliver a message, it probably can be established whether or not he has done his duty. In other situations it's not as easy. For example, sometimes it is not easy to determine when one has a duty to respond to an appeal for a donation."

"Is there a connection between judgments about deserts and motives?" wondered Mae.

"Yes," replied Bill, "I believe there is a direct connection between *deserts* and *motives*. A person deserves an approval or reward for wanting to do what is right and deserves disapproval or punishment for being indifferent as to whether his action is the right thing to do. In other words, judgments about desert take into account motives."

Mae was still uneasy about Pinker's view of just desert when he claims that it involves a sense of revenge. Pinker's view, in her mind, failed to show a connection between desert and motive.

But, it was time to return to their classes.

A day later ...

When Bill and Mae met the next day for lunch, Bill was ready with his question, "How do young people view the concept of desert according to Brooks?"

"The young people in the article by Brooks do not seem to distinguish the moral sense from the non-moral sense," maintained Mae. "When they were asked, in a recent study, to identify a moral dilemma they had faced, two-thirds of them either couldn't answer the question or shifted to describing problems that are not moral. They would not expect a person to offer reasons why someone deserves a punishment or reward. Individual tastes are reason enough."

"They probably would agree that approvals are not wilful," observed Bill. "An attitude of approval is not something one has wilfully."

"The young people show little interest in any form of punishment or reward," remarked Mae. "What's more, they maintain that a person does not deserve a reward because all acts are a matter of personal preference. The only bad acts acknowledged by the young people are crimes such as rape or murder," observed Mae. "Even when considering things like drunk driving, cheating in school or cheating on a partner, moral thinking doesn't enter the picture for them according to the study reviewed by Brooks."

"In fact," Bill observed, "the young people pay little attention to desert because they focus on the self."

"As they view it," noted Mae, "a person does not deserve punishment for willing to do wrong or for planning to commit a wrong act."

"How would you describe their view of authorities?" asked Bill.

"I think they believe that the true self is whatever is most natural; they try to follow that authentic inner self whatever that means," replied Mae.

"What do you think about their view?" asked Bill.

"I find it troubling," said Mae. "It offers nothing more than personal preferences - it offers no directions for life. I wonder if Brooks offers any information on why young people take this view of morality."

In frustration, the conversation came to an abrupt end ... both had nothing more to add. So, they returned to their classes.

The young people as understood by Bill and Mae certainly reflect a different view of desert than the position taken in this book. More on this later. Having added *desert* to *duty*, *rights* and *motive*, once again, has created an increasingly complex context for resolving moral dilemmas. That takes us to the last category in the Principled Thinking Model, *justice*, which is discussed in the following Chapter.

Chapter 9
Justice

Conceptual Framework

The concept of *justice* provides a context for integrating the concepts which have been explained so far: duties, rights, motive and desert. *Justice* refers to the distribution of what people want or do not want. For example, in the preface Grandma encouraged her grandsons to be fair. That's why she asked Tommy to share some of his pennies with Billy.

This Chapter explains how the concept of justice integrates the following concepts:
- Act from a desire to do one's *duty*
- Recognize a person's *rights*
- Act from a morally good *motive*
- Give people what they *deserve*
- Act with impartiality in pursuit of *justice*

For a complete list of the questions and statements about *justice*, go to Figure 9.

Justice also includes the terms *just, fair,* and *equitable,* as well as their antonyms *unjust, unfair,* and *inequitable*[95]. These terms are frequently used in moral and legal philosophy.

Key words

People judge many things to be *just* or *unjust*. They judge actions when they say, "That was the only just thing to do". Sometimes laws are judged to be unjust. This applies to legal codes. When a person is judged to have been punished excessively, people say that the person was treated unfairly. Sometimes it is said of a person that "He received his just desert" which is to say that he got what he deserved, be it an object of interest or disinterest. Judges are sometimes accused of pronouncing unjust judgments. Members of a family sometimes feel that the disbursement of the family estate was unjust. Reformers frequently argue that the economy of a country is unjust towards the poor. Historically, some religions have made a distinction between just and unjust wars. Politicians have claimed that, if elected, they will usher in a just society. Governments are sometimes accused of being unjust to certain segments of the population. Leaders of reform movements sometimes claim that their just cause warrants interference in the orderly flow of society. Appeals are sometimes made for a just distribution of the limited resources of a nation.

Applying *justice* to people introduces a usage of this term that is different from all the others. It does not refer to the same thing as applied to an action, law or sentence. Justice as applied to a person makes reference to motive. When justice is used in this way, it is used in a way good or virtuous are used to refer to the motive of a person. In other words, for a person to be considered a good person it is not sufficient that he make just or fair allocation. For example, in the Preface, Grandma wanted Tommy to be a good boy by sharing some of his pennies with his brother If Tommy had shared some of his pennies with Billy after Grandma had threatened to take all of Tommy's pennies if he would not share some of them with Billy, Tommy would have done what Grandma asked him to do. However, he would have done it out of fear of losing all his pennies if he did not do as Grandma asked him to do.

All the other uses of the term justice listed above do not make reference to motives but only to the objective characteristics of what is judged to be just. The objective sense of the term *just* makes reference to the rightness of an act. When *just* is used with reference to the distribution of goods, for example, it is used in a way that *justice* refers to *right*. Hence, *just* is frequently treated as being interchangeable with *right*. However, that usage fails to take into account the distinctive characteristics of *just* discussed later in this Chapter.

Usually *justice* is used in the more narrow sense where it refers to the decisions and actions of people who possess some kind of authority or the right to supervise the activities of other people. This usage is reflected in the reference to just laws, just punishment, just allocation, and so on. For example, the sentence pronounced by a judge on a person who has been convicted of a crime may be just or unjust.

I mentioned two other terms that belong to the class of justice: *fair* and *equitable*. *Fair* may be used in the objective and subjective sense as is the case with *just*. The objective sense is reflected in the statement "He did the only fair thing". The subjective sense is meant when it is said of a person, "He is a fair person."

The only difference between *fair* and *just* is the context in which they are used. As I mentioned above, *just* is commonly used with reference to the decisions and acts made by people in authority such as government officials and judges. *Fair* is used in less formal situations. For example, it is often said that a teacher is not fair to a certain child. *Fair* also seems to be used in situations where the person who is making the judgment is involved in the distribution of objects in trust. For example, teachers need to be fair to the children who have been entrusted to their care.

Equitable is used only in the objective sense. It is used commonly for the distribution of objects of interest or disinterest. Essentially, *equitable* describes the distribution. For example, Grandma wanted the grandsons to have equal number of pennies because she wanted to be fair to both grandsons.

In the objective sense, *just* refers to the distribution or allocation of objects of interest or disinterest. For example, a disbursement of funds is just or unjust depending on how the money (object of interest) is distributed or allocated. Laws are just or unjust depending on how they distribute or allocate legal obligations (objects of disinterest) and legal rights (objects of interest). Governments are just or unjust depending on whether they legislate and execute just or unjust laws. Societies are just or unjust depending on how the objects of interest (property, services) and objects of disinterest (taxes, military service) are allocated or distributed. Judges make judgments about distributing or allocating objects of interest or disinterest.

There are certain elements that must be part of the objective sense of the term *justice*. First, there has to be a *distributor* who allocates objects of interest or disinterest. For example, when a judge pronounces a sentence, the judge allocates of an object of disinterest. The distributor, in this case, the judge, must be a moral person in order to make a just distribution.

Second, a judgment about justice requires a *recipient*. A criminal is the recipient of an object of disinterest. It would seem that although a recipient need not be a moral person, he could be an actual or potential moral person. He probably has objects of interest and disinterest.

Third, there has to be a *distribution*. The distribution of an object of interest or disinterest is not *just* based only on what the recipient deserves. Whether a distribution is just depends on the duty of the distributor, the rights of the recipient, the motive of the distributor, and what the recipient deserves.

Key ideas

Not all right acts are considered just. For example, it may be right to lend your math textbook to a friend but it does not follow that it is wrong not to lend your math textbook to someone. Even though it may be right, the just or right thing to do may be to tell your friend to purchase his own textbook. But, *all right acts are just.* It seems confusing to claim that a certain act is just even though it is wrong. One of the conditions for an act to be just is that it must be right. For example, if it is just to help all of the children in class with their math, it would also be the right thing to do. On the other hand, if it is wrong to help some children with their math while they are writing a math exam, it would also be unjust to the rest of the class.

Not all wrong acts are unjust. When John Doe took a wrong turn on the way to the airport and missed his flight, he did not commit an unjust act. If he took a deliberate wrong turn out of spite so that his sister would miss her flight, it would be wrong. All unjust acts are wrong.

In short, the relationship between right and just as well as wrong and unjust can be summarized as follows:

- Not all right acts are just but all just acts are right.
- Not all wrong acts are unjust but all unjust acts are wrong

An *act of distributing or allocating an object of interest or disinterest is not fair only from the point of view of its utility.* Some people believe that fairness includes utility. For example, some people argue that promoting justice through the courts brings with it the utility of law and order for society. However, this apparent correlation between fairness and utility does not always seem to follow. For example, suppose longer sentences are an effective way of reducing crime for males ages 35-65. Should all men of this age therefore receive longer sentences? Should the father in this age range, who has children who depend on him to provide shelter and food for them, receive a longer sentence just because of his age? In other words, should factors other than age also be considered in the length of a sentence to be fair to everyone affected by a sentence? These questions raise doubts about the apparent correlation between fairness and utility."

Is a distribution considered just or unjust from the point of view of the interests of the recipient? Not necessarily. Objects of needs are objects of interest, but not all objects of interests are needed. Sometimes whatever is distributed is something people want but do not need. Sometimes the distribution involves objects of disinterest.

Is a distribution considered just or unjust from the point of view of the rights of the recipient? Although the rights of the recipient should be considered, rights do not offer a sufficient reason. For example, Mr. Smith may have a right to see his doctor at the appointed time about a headache but the doctor may have a duty to first attend to a patient who requires immediate emergency surgery.

A *distribution can affect the recipients* in one of three ways. First, a distribution does not favor one recipient over others. Second, the distribution favors one recipient over others on the basis of sound principles or reasons. Third, the distribution favors one or some recipients over others without sound principles or reasons. Which of these characteristics must a distribution have in order for the distribution to be just? The first possibility (i.e., the distribution does not favor one recipients over others) does not involve the issue of just distribution but involves only the impartiality of the distributor which will be discussed later. The second alternative involves the issue of justice because the decision is made on the basis of sound principles or reasons. The third option may not be just because a distribution is unjust if it favors one recipient over others without sound principles or reasons.

Is a distribution considered just or unjust from the point of view of motives? That could not be the case because any reference to motives clearly is a reference to the distributor and not to that which is distributed.

After all these objections to what constitutes a just distribution, I offer the following explanation of a just distribution: *A distribution is just or unjust from the point of view of the way it affects the interests of recipients relative to one another including those who should be considered recipients.* For example, in a case where a judge has to determine what constitutes a just sentence, she has to take into account how people, who committed a similar offence, were treated. Of course the similarity between cases has to take into account all extenuating circumstance such as the mental health of the recipient, the impact of the crime on the victims, the context in which the crime was committed and so on. Whether in fact, a distribution affects recipients as anticipated is a different matter. What people do must not be confused with what they should do.

For a distribution to be just, a second condition must be met. The distribution must be made by a distributor who is *impartial.* Impartiality in the primary sense, applies to the person making the distribution whereas justice refers to the distribution itself. To say that a distributor is impartial is to say that the distributor favors one recipient over others based on sound principles or reasons.

That a distribution must be done with impartiality in order for it to be a just distribution raises the question: *Are all distributions done with impartiality just?* Not necessarily. For example, suppose a college admissions officer applies the admissions regulations to all applicants without checking whether the applicants are able to pay the admission fee. The admissions officer was impartial but his action was not necessarily just given that some applicants were unable to pay due to circumstances beyond their control. The admissions officer was impartial, yet the distribution favored one or some recipients without sound principles or reasons. Sometimes people use the reference to impartiality as evidence to support the contention that a distribution is just. The admissions officer probably would insist that his action was just because he was impartial in administering the regulation. There are no general rules for determining whether a person is impartial. Each case must be considered on its own merits. Statements about whether a distributor is impartial are descriptive and not normative.

For a distribution to be just, several conditions must be met: The distributor must have a right to make the distributions for it is wrong for someone to distribute something if he does not have a right to do it. Also, the distributor must have a duty to make a distribution. Lastly, since only moral persons can have a duty to make a moral judgment, the distributor must be a moral person.

If a person deserved a reward, granting it (i.e., object of interest) would be just, Similarly, it would be just to inflict punishment if it is deserved. Allocating a reward or inflicting a punishment must take into account the way in which the distribution of objects of interest and disinterest affect the interests and needs of the recipients relative to one another. Hence, judgments about whether an act is just must take into account what a person deserves.

When is discrimination unjust? Discrimination is unjust when a person has a duty not to discriminate or when it is wrong to discriminate. For example, since it is wrong to discriminate against a person on the basis of color, it is unjust. However, not every act of discrimination is wrong. In fact, it may be wrong not to discriminate in some situations. It may be wrong in some situation not to discriminate in favour of the disadvantaged. For example, it would be wrong not to discriminate in favour of a single mom working for minimum wages to have access to subsidized child care.

It is possible for a person to deserve punishment and yet for it not to be just for someone to mete out that punishment. Suppose the children in a rural school gather at their one-room school one morning when the teacher is too sick to come to school. Suppose that one of the older boys picks on one of the younger boys by calling him names. The older boy deserves punishment even though there is nobody around who has the right to punish him. In this case the judgment is still just; it is made in terms of conceiving of a person who would have the right to punish the older boy. In fact, in most every-day situations, nobody has the right to punish others.

I need to draw attention to the difference between *retribution* and *retributive justice*. Retribution refers to acts of taking revenge or harming someone in retaliation for some harm that the person has done. Suppose Jim springs a surprise attack on David on his way to school because David won a fight with Jim a week ago after school. Jim's action would be considered retribution for something David did to Jim. Retributive justice, on the other hand, refers to the just allocation of objects of disinterest. A judge exercises retributive justice when he sentences a convicted person to a just sentence. In this case, the judge allocates an object of disinterest.

So far, I have defined justice in terms of two or more people. That raises the question: *How can the distribution of an object of interest or disinterest to one individual be just?* The distribution to one person could be just if the distributor would decide to make the same distribution of objects of interest or disinterest to all persons in similar situations. Suppose, one of the students in a math class, Sophie, is not able to purchase a notebook for math. She deserves a notebook to do her math assignments; the notebook is an object of interest for her. The principal of the school decides to give Sophie a notebook because he has the right to distribute school supplies to needy students in his school. He justifies his action of giving a notebook to one student on the basis that he would do it for any student in his school who cannot afford to purchase school supplies.

This concludes a review of the five categories of the Principled Thinking Model – duty, rights, motive, desert, and justice - and related concepts for making moral judgments about right and wrong. The review shows how they are needed to decide whether an act is just or fair. Figure 9 identifies the five categories of the Principled Thinking Model and the key concepts in each category. .

Concepts about Justice	Responses
1. Justice refers to the distribution of objects of interest or disinterest.	
2. Justice should be administered by people who exercise authority	
3. Fair may be used in the objective and subjective sense	
4. What is the relationship between right acts and just acts?	- Not all right acts are just but all just acts are right - Not all wrong acts are unjust but all unjust acts are wrong

5. On what basis is a distribution just or unjust?	It depends on how the distribution affects the interests of the recipients relative to each other.
6. Are these factors sufficient to determine whether an act is just? - the recipient's desert - its utility - the needs of the recipient - the rights of the recipient - the motive of the distributor	 Not sufficient Not sufficient Not sufficient Not sufficient Not sufficient
7. Impartiality refers to the distributor.	
8. A just act is an act of impartiality.	
9. The issue of justice includes:	- A distributor - A distribution of objects of interest or disinterest - A recipient
10. For a person to be impartial he must favor one recipient over others based on sound principles or reasons.	
11. A distribution which is made with impartiality may be just or unjust.	Impartiality does not ensure that an act is just.
12. It may be wrong in some cases not to discriminate.	A just distribution may require discrimination in some cases
13. For a distribution to be just, the distributor must meet the following conditions:	- have the right to make the distribution - have a duty to make the distribution - be a moral person

14. Is it possible for a just act ever to be wrong?	No
15. Is it possible for a person to deserve punishment and yet for it not to be just for someone to punish that person?	Yes. Nobody present may have the right and authority to punish that person
16. What is retribution?	Retribution is an act of revenge or harming someone in retaliation
17. What is retributive justice?	It is the just allocation of objects of disinterest.
18. How is it possible for the allocation of an object of disinterest to be an act of impartiality?	To say that a distributor is impartial is to say that the distributor does not favor one recipient over others without sound principles or reasons.
19. How can the allocation of an object of interest or disinterest to one individual be just?	It can be just if the distributor would decide to make the same distribution of objects of interest or disinterest to all persons in similar situations.
20. What is involved in the pursuit of justice?	- Act from a desire to do one's duty - Recognize a person's rights - Act from a morally good motive - Give people what they deserve - Make just decisions - Act with impartiality in pursuit of justice.

Figure 9: Justice

Young people's view of justice

The young people's view of duty, rights, motive and desert has already been described. As has been mentioned before, these categories are an integral part of the concept of justice. In this section, I will focus on the features unique to justice. Before I do so, here are highlights of what duty, rights, motive and desert mean to young people as viewed by Brooks. First, they insist that a person does not have a *duty* or any sense of obligation. For them there is no conflict of duties. Second, *rights* are a matter of looking after your own interests. Personal feelings are the guide for what is right and wrong. . They do not make a clear distinction between duties and rights; both are personal. Third, they claim that moral choices are just a matter of individual taste; they do not include morally good *motives* as a necessary condition for an act to be morally good. They maintain believing that an act is right is a sufficient motive for doing it. They do not differentiate between morally good motives and naturally good motives. They do not believe that people desire to do wrong for the sake of doing wrong. Fourth, they do not expect a person to offer reasons for making the claim that someone *deserves* a punishment or reward. They show little interest in any form of punishment or rewards. The only bad acts acknowledged by them are crimes of rape or murder.

In short, the young people as described by Brooks take a consistent view across all four categories: duty, rights, motive and desert; their view is "It's personal. Who am I to say?"

Similarly, they take a personal or subjective view of justice. They approach all authorities with a subjective view be they parents, lawyers, legislators, law enforcement officers, or any other person in a position of authority. An objective sense of *justice* is not considered. They hold the same view of fair and equitable. A person does not have to be able to distinguish right from wrong. A distribution need not favor the needs or interests of one recipient over others on the basis of sound principles or reasons.

A distributor need not be impartial. Impartiality does not necessarily ensure that an act is just. They would agree that there are no general rules for determining whether a person is impartial; each case is up to the individual. A person need not have a right to make a distribution since making the distribution is up to the individual. Nor does the distributor have to have a duty to make a distribution.

In the view of the young people as reviewed by Brooks, duty, rights, motive, desert, and impartiality are not necessary to resolve moral dilemmas in pursuit of justice. In the Introduction, I drew attention to Daniel Kahneman's[96] reference to system 2 thinking or deep thinking which he considers essential for thinking through complex moral issues. The young people in the study did not see a need for deep thinking.

At the same time, the young people draw our attention to the power of personal feeling in the form of empathy. Brooks points out that "There have been some positive outcomes from this focus. Women, minorities and the poor, who traditionally were considered inferior and often were humiliated, have achieved a sense of self-esteem from this focus on universal rights[97]." These various groups bonded through a strong sentiment of fellow feeling for each other. This emotional bond carried them through years of discrimination till some of their rights were acknowledged.

Conversation about justice - Mae and Bill

Once again, let's return to Mae and Bill to see how they understand the concept of justice. Do they incorporate the concepts of duties, rights, motives and desert into the concept of justice? Mae was still determined to get clarification on the concept of *just desert*. Pinker's[98] view that somehow justice is a form of revenge continued to trouble her. So she wanted to dig deeper into the concept of justice.

She started the conversation by rambling about how people judge many things to be just or unjust. She recalled expressions like, *that was the only just thing to do, he received his just desert*, and *just society*. "How could the notion of justice include revenge?" she wondered.

Bill interjected, "Justice as applied to a person is about a person's motive. This subjective sense of the term justice applies only to people."

Mae got it; so she added, "When justice is used in this way, it is used in a way similar to the way *good* or *virtuous* are used. They refer to the motive of a person."

Expanding on it, Bill maintained, "In fact, for a person to be considered a morally good person, it is not sufficient that he make right decisions. Should a person do so out of fear or self-interest, he or she would not be regarded as a morally good person. A person must do so from a morally good motive." Bill continued by explaining the second usage of justice, "All other references to justice make reference to the objective sense, whether an act is right. It is used in a way that right refers to duties. Hence, justice frequently is treated as being interchangeable with the term right."

'Wow,' exclaimed Mae. "So justice includes the concept of motive and duty. Let's explore these relationships some more. Are all right acts just?" she asked.

"No," replied Bill. "For an act to be just, it must meet two conditions. The act must be right and it must be done from a morally good motive."

"It's still confusing to me. Can you give me an example?" asked Mae.

"OK, here's one," replied Bill. "Suppose John assisted an older person to cross the street safely hoping that he would receive a tip. John did the right thing but not for a morally good motive in that he was hoping for a reward. John acted selfishly and not from a morally good motive."

"Interesting," observed Mae and then reversed the question, "Are all just acts right?"

To which Bill replied, "Of course, just acts are right because they need to be right to be just. If John had assisted an older person to cross the street because he wanted to make sure she would cross the street safely, his action would have been just because he would have met the two conditions for an act to be just."

Mae continued, "Are all wrong acts unjust?"

"Not necessarily," replied Bill. "Suppose Betty does not take her medication as prescribed by her doctor. The act would be wrong but not unjust. She was not duty-bound to follow the doctor's orders."

Again Mae asked the reverse question, "Are all unjust acts wrong?"

"It would be a contradiction to claim that an act is unjust but nevertheless right," insisted Bill. "When an act is unjust, it is wrong. Suppose my friend and I both fail to make a payment on the parking meter and appear before a judge to plead not guilty for forgetting to pay for parking. Suppose the judge fines my friend $45.00 and fines me $95.00 for the same first time offense. I would argue that the judge was unjust or unfair in fining me more than my friend. I would rightly argue that is wrong because it is wrong to fine one person more than another for the same offense. I repeat – if an act is unjust it is wrong. That's only logical."

"Does justice include desert?" asked Mae.

"Possibly, though not necessarily," replied Bill. "In the case where John helped an elderly person cross the street safely, she did not deserve to be helped by John. Nor did John deserve a reward. However, when a bully on the playground injures another person, the bully deserves to be punished."

Mae was wondering about the utility or outcome of an act. So she asked, "Is an act fair from the point of view of its utility?"

On first thought, that seemed plausible to Bill. However, he wondered, "That would suggest that the end justifies the means. It could lead to some very unjust actions. Suppose a student, who stole another student's lunch just before Christmas, was suspended for the rest of the school year to discourage students from stealing. That would seem unjust (excessive punishment) even if it might discourage some students from stealing. In this case, the end would not justify the means even though some students might be deterred from stealing."

"Often, we use fair instead of just," observed Mae. "Can we use 'fair' in the objective and subjective sense?"

"Yes. In the objective sense, we say, 'That was the only fair thing to do'. In the subjective sense, we say, 'She is a fair person," replied Bill.

"Justice and fairness are not used quite in the same way," Mae pointed out. "Justice commonly refers to the decisions and acts of people in authority such as government officials or a judge. Fair is used in situations that involve individuals. For example, we say that a teacher is not fair with one of her students."

Bill added, "The term, equitable, is used only in the objective sense. It is used to describe a distribution of likes and dislikes. Essentially, *equitable* describes a distribution. When my friends and I play the game, Monopoly, we make sure that everyone starts the game with the same amount of money. We count everyone's money to make sure that the allocation of money is equitable."

"How is justice used in the objective sense?" asked Mae.

"The objective sense of justice refers to the distribution of likes and dislikes," replied Bill and he went on to give some examples, "The disbursement of funds is just or unjust depending on how the funds are distributed. Laws are just or unjust depending on how they allocate legal obligations and legal rights."

To which, Mae added, "I get it. Governments are just or unjust depending on whether they legislate just or unjust laws; and societies are just or unjust depending on how civic services are allocated and taxes are levied."

"Of course, there has to be a distributor," maintained Bill. "The distributor must be a moral person for a distribution to be fair."

"The recipient need not be a moral person," interjected Mae.

"Agreed. But, the distribution of likes and dislikes is not based only on what the recipient deserves," cautioned Bill.

"Of course, there has to be a distribution," added Mae.

This discussion about distribution prompted Bill to revisit the question, "Is a distribution fair from the point of view of its utility? Many people seem to believe that justice includes utility."

Mae didn't think so, "The correlation between justice and utility does not always follow even though some people believe that fairness includes utility. Some feel that promoting justice through the courts brings with it the utility of law and order for society. However, this apparent correlation between fairness and utility does not always seem to follow. For example, suppose longer sentences are an effective way of reducing crime for males ages 35-65. Should all men of this age therefore receive longer sentences? Should the man in this age range, whose children depend on their father to provide shelter and food for them, receive a longer sentence than other men not in this age group? In other words, should factors other than age also be considered in the length of a sentence to be fair to everyone? These questions raise doubts about the apparent correlation between fairness and utility.

"Is a distribution considered just or unjust from the point of view of the needs of the recipient?" asked Mae.

"Objects of needs are objects of interest, but not all objects of interest are needed," Bill reminded Mae. "Sometimes I want what I do not need."

"What about the rights of the recipient?" asked Mae.

To which Bill replied, "Although the rights of the recipient need to be considered, the recipient's rights do not offer a sufficient reason for an act to be just. Try this example. While twelve year old Sammy is doing his math homework, his mother is reading her favorite novel. Sammy is frustrated because he does not understand his math assignment. Although his mother has every right to read, she probably feels she should interrupt her reading and help Sammy solve his math problem. Since that would be the right thing to do and she believes that it is the right thing to do, it would also be the just thing to do even though this action would interfere with his mother's right to read her novel.

Bill shifted to talking about motive by asking, "Is a distribution considered just or unjust based on motive? That could not be the case. Does it matter whether I want to be fair or just when I grade my students' math tests? Any reference to motives would clearly be a reference to the distributor and not to that which is distributed," Mae pointed out. "In your example, you are actually referring to yourself as the distributor."

Mae was ready to express her view of justice. "I think" announced Mae, "a distribution is just or unjust from the point of view of the way in which it affects the interests of recipients relative to one another including those who should be considered recipients."

Once again, Bill was impressed but he wanted to explore justice further. So he asked, "What if a distributor (i.e., a teacher) favors one recipient (i.e., a student) over other students? Does that make his action unjust?'

"Not necessarily; maybe one student needs to be favoured," replied Mae. "Maybe one of the classmates is an immigrant who is just learning the language used in class and needs more help to understand what the teacher is saying. "Never-the-less, the impartiality of the distributor is important. To say that a distributor is impartial is to say that the distributor favors one recipients over others *based on sound principles or reasons*." Mae placed special emphasis on *based on sound principles or reasons*.

"Unfortunately," Bill maintains, "it seems to me there are no general rules for determining whether a person is impartial. I think each case must be considered on its own merits."

To which, Mae added, "Statements about whether a distributor is impartial are descriptive and not normative. They describe how a decision was made; not whether a decision was right or wrong."

"Interesting," observed Bill.

"Watch out," warned Mae, "Whether a distribution affects recipients as anticipated is a different matter. Keep in mind that what people do must not be confused with what they should do or think they should do."

Once again, Mae observed the connection between justice and the other categories. She pointed out, "The distributor must have a right to make a distribution, have a duty to make the distribution, take into account the motive of the distributor, take into account what a person deserves, and consider whether an act is just."

"I couldn't have said it better," said Bill. "But, can a discriminatory distribution ever be just?" wondered Bill. "I recognize that it is unjust to discriminate against a person on the basis of the color of his skin." But he repeated, "Is it ever unjust not to discriminate?"

This question reminded Mae of what John Rawls had to say about justice. She paraphrased Rawls[99], "If you need to favour one party over against another, favour the least favoured." To which she added the obvious, "It would be unjust to favour the most favoured."

Bill came up with another question, "Is it possible for a just act ever to be wrong?"

Mae was clear about her response to this one. With a firm voice, she replied, "NO, it would be contradictory to say that a just act is wrong. Every act that is just is also right and every act that is unjust is also wrong."

One more tricky question from Bill, "Is it possible for a person to deserve punishment and yet for it not to be just for someone to punish that person?"

In response, Mae asked Bill to consider this situation, "Suppose the children in a rural school gather at their one-room school one morning when the teacher is too sick to come to school. Suppose that one of the older boys picks on one of the younger boys by calling him names. Does the older boy deserve punishment even though nobody was around who had the authority to punish him?"

The answer was obvious to Bill, "Of course the older boy's action was wrong and he deserved punishment. Had the teacher been around, he would likely have punished the older boy."

Mae could not resist responding with a logical argument, "To say that someone deserves something is to say that it would be just to administer some form of reward or punishment to that person by some conceivable person who has the authority to do so." To which she added, "In fact, in most situations, nobody has the right to punish others."

Bill did not respond.

Before time was running out, Bill fired one more difficult question, "How can the distribution of likes and dislikes be fair to one individual? I can see how allocating the same number of candies to two or more children can be done fairly."

Mae did not respond to the question. She felt the urge to explore the place that empathy has in the pursuit of justice. Somehow a strictly rational perspective on resolving moral dilemmas seemed insufficient for her. So she posed this scenario. "Suppose I need to decide what to say to a parent whose child has been found stealing a lunch from another student in our school. I might ask myself, 'What if I was the parent, who received a call from my child's school, about my child having stolen another student's lunch. How would I want the teacher to talk to me about it? In other words, I would put myself in the shoes of the mother whom I have to call. Might this role exchange prompt me to be more considerate, even empathic, towards the parent and the student?" Mae looked stressed when she added, "How might that influence my reflection on what I might say to the parent?"

Bill conceded but insisted that Mae's example is simply an exception. He offered a different situation, "Jim, one of my grade nine students, was absent from school two consecutive days. When I asked for an explanation upon his return to school, he said he had gone fishing with some friends. How should I respond to him?" Bill was sure this example would put an end to Mae's bleeding heart sense of fairness.

Mae responded with another situation, "Remember," she said, "the time last year when David, one of my students, attended a concert with his parents? I raised this situation in a staff meeting to get some guidance on what to do about the student's absence. Most of the staff insisted that I should not chastise David for his absence, but that I should insist that he complete the assignment he had missed for homework. I think the staff felt that I should be considerate and not simply treat David's absence as truancy even though he had not informed the school that he would be absent. Does the way I handled this case make any sense to you?"

Bill conceded that the new case was something he would consider, though, he quickly added that he did not intend to be quite as considerate as Mae had been with David.

Mae thought of another situation quite different for the last two. She described it this way, "I recall an incident where Helen, one of my students, missed a final English exam. Again, she had taken the problem of what to do about Helen's absence to a staff meeting. Several questions were raised. Why had Helen missed the exam? Should Mae be expected to prepare a new exam for Helen? How similar should the two exams be? Could Mae arrive at a year-end grade for Helen without requiring her to take an exam? Before long, one staff member, Ms Daley, insisted this issue was a matter of principle. So she asked, 'Should we allow one student obtain a year-end grade by averaging her performance throughout the year, but require everyone else to sink or swim based on their performance on a final exam? How is that fair?' To which another teacher countered, 'How is it fair for the teacher to prepare a separate exam for one student and ensure that it is equally difficult to the exam taken by the rest of the students in her class?"

Mae posed the question to Bill, "Which principle should take precedence over the other: being fair to the student who missed the exam or being fair to the teacher?

Bill wasn't sure but he saw Mae's point and he conceded that being considerate should be part of the decision.

However, Bill could not resist challenging Mae with another situation. "I recall," he said, "a situation where a parent refused to provide her child's school with their home address and telephone number. The school refused to register the child." He asked Mae, "Should the school have registered the child?"

Mae felt this question had no clear answer. Her first impulse was to ask herself, "Should a school deny access to a local school to children in the neighbourhood when parents will not or cannot submit a home address and telephone number? What if no parent provided this basic information? How could the school operate?"

Bill was clear about his position on this one. So he maintained, "No home address and telephone number means no access. I do not see the need to consider the universal consequences of many children not submitting their home address and phone number. That's an absurd probability."

Mae expanded on her point by adding, "To pursue justice, people need to consider a situation from different perspectives. This could include engaging in a role exchange or considering an issue by looking at it in the context of a new case. What if I had a child, lost my home and became homeless? Does that mean my daughter could not attend school ... any school? I kind of feel some empathy for the parent we were discussing."

Bill was surprised. He realized the significance of what Mae had just said.

A day later ...

When they met again for lunch the next day, Bill changed the conversation to exploring how young people understand the concept of justice by asking, "What is the view of justice held by the young people as reported by Brooks?"

"The young people take a personal or subjective view of justice," said Mae. "They don't simply assume that people in a position of authority such as parents, lawyers, legislators, and law enforcement officers are just."

"Do they accept the objective sense of justice in some situations?" asked Bill.

"No," replied Mae, "because right and wrong is simply up to the individual."

Bill was wondering about the utility or outcome of an act. So he asked, "Do they consider an act as being fair from the point of view of its outcome or utility?"

On first thought, that seemed plausible. Mae wondered, "That would suggest that the end justifies the means. They might accept that view."

"What about considering justice from the point of view of the needs or interests of the recipient?" asked Bill.

"For them," responded Mae, "the needs of the recipient are sufficient because whether a distribution is considered just or unjust is up to each individual."

"Is the motive of the distributor relevant for them?" Bob asked.

"No," replied Mae, "The motive of the person who hands out a reward or punishes a person does not determine whether an act is just. Only the recipient's interests are relevant."

"Do sound principles or reasons have any place in justifying an act?" asked Bob.

"Since distributions are personal," said Mae, "sound principles or reasons are not needed to favor the needs of one person over another. For them, all distributions are simply personal."

"It follows," says Bill, "that a distributor need not be impartial."

Let me see if I got this right," said Mae. "For them a distributor need not have a right to make a distribution nor does she have a duty to make a distribution. The motive of the distributor is immaterial. Whether a recipient deserves anything is entirely up to the recipient. Did I get that right?"

"So it seems," replied Bill. "Whether an act is just depends entirely on each individual. And," Bill added, "discrimination are neither just or unjust because all decisions are personal."

"How would you sum up the view of the young people?" asked Mae.

"As I understand Brooks, they place great emphasis on personal happiness," replied Bill. "They focus on maximizing pleasant experiences and avoiding pain and vulnerability. I feel the researcher overstates this focus. If he had asked questions about having empathy for other people in distress, the young people probably would have shown a sense of empathy in cases they could recall."

That was it; they had to return to their classes. Was Mae more comfortable with Pinker's claim that the notion of justice includes revenge? We will never know. What do you think?

Empathy is mostly missing from the focus on the use of the language that facilitates critical thinking as presented in the Principled Thinking Model advanced in this book. The critical place of a sense of empathy to resolve moral dilemmas in pursuit of justice or fairness is discussed in Part II. A sense of empathy does not replace the Principled Thinking Model but serves as an essential complement.

Part II

Resolving moral dilemmas in pursuit of justice requires a sense of empathy or fellow feeling

Although this book is focused primarily on the thinking necessary to resolve moral dilemmas, I draw attention to the context in which the thinking must take place. The context, which has been addressed by philosophers David Hume[100], John Rawls[101] and Nel Nodding[102] and psychologist Carol Gilligan[103] refers to the emotional setting essential for resolving moral dilemmas. The emotional setting, they agree, is a sense of empathy or fellow feeling necessary to urge people to resolve moral dilemmas.

Chapter 10 offers a brief review of the studies conducted by philosophers and psychologists who contend that resolving moral dilemmas requires not only critical thinking but also an emotive sense of empathy. Chapter 11 shows how a sense of empathy can be prompted by moral values principle tests to create cognitive dissonance and possibly resolve moral dilemmas. Chapter 12 identifies different forms of dissonance and emphasizes that cognitive dissonance is the most likely to facilitate the resolution of moral dilemmas.

Chapter 10
Cognition and the Affect

This Chapter addresses the concern raised by Mae about her unease in relying totally on rational decision making to resolve moral dilemmas. She felt that a sense of fellow feeling or empathy is needed to resolve moral dilemmas through activities such as role exchange or considering new similar cases. Many philosophers and psychologists support Mae's contention that, although moral decisions require moral thinking, it is not sufficient to make just decisions. A sense of empathy is needed.

In *Treatise of Human Nature*[104], David Hume stressed the importance of the sentiment of humanity (fellow feeling) to place reason in proper perspective to resolve moral issues. In fact, Hume claimed that "sentiment is the driving force of our moral lives whereas reasoning is biased and impotent, fit primarily to be a servant of the passions[205]." Sentiments give us pleasure when we encounter virtue and displeasure when we encounter vice. At the same time, he recognized the importance of reasons in connection with sentiments. Both, reason and sentiment concur in almost all moral determinations.

In *Theory of Justice*[106]" John Rawls maintains that our ability to create a just and fair society is tied directly to how fully we empathize with others especially with the least fortunate. By applying the *difference principle*[107], he explains that those with greater natural capacity or merit need not be stripped of their distinction. Never-the-less the focus should be on favoring the least fortunate. This view reflects a unique concept of equality which does not include leveling inequality; instead it involves sharing one another's fate with a focus on the common benefit. Rawls presents his concept of justice in the form of thought experiments. He offers no assurance that his theory of justice will ultimately be applied by any individuals or institutions.

Philosopher, Nel Nodding, emphasises the importance of a reciprocal relationship between the one-caring and the one-cared-for in her book, *Caring*[108] which is illustrated in Figure 10 below. The relationship between the one caring and the one cared for is one of receptivity by both parties. Although decision making is rational, receptivity is a non-rational relationship called *caring* which includes a feeling of inclusion by both parties. The one cared for can express receptivity through direct response, expressing delight and showing growth. A caring relationship can take the form of *natural responsiveness* or *ethical responsibility* for behaving as the one caring or the one cared for. The former reflects a parent-child relationship and the later reflects the relationship between strangers. The foundation of moral behaviour is feeling or *sentiment*. Hence the one caring pays close attention to the development of the one cared for. Moral statements are derived from that caring attitude. This is how Nodding describes the relationship, "A caring relationship requires the engrossment and motivational displacement of the one caring, and it requires the recognition and spontaneous response of the one cared for[109].

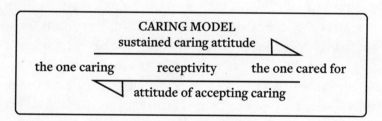

Figure 10: Caring Model

Through her moving case studies, psychologist, Carol Gilligan, *In a Different* Voice[110] , maintains that morality is based on a caring relationships coupled with the principle of fairness. She refers to it as "a dialogue between fairness and caring ... which gives rise to a more comprehensive portrayal of adult work and family relationships[111]." Her studies, which are based on the development of women, conclude with an appeal to understanding development in the context of men and women. Hence, her focus is on fairness and caring which combines men's focus on fairness and women's focus on caring.

How would these philosophers and psychologists address the following scenario.

> The parent of a child, who had been sick for some time and had continued her education at her own pace, requested that their child be allowed to skip a grade to be with children who were learning at their daughter's level. In other words, the parents felt their child had matured more than her peers in her present class. The parents were concerned that their child would get bored with school work and might lose interest in school if she is not challenged. The counselors and administrators denied the parent's request and patronized the parents by claiming that professional parents tend to push their children and over-estimate their children's abilities.

First and foremost, David Hume would encourage the counselors and administrators to sense how the parents feel about their daughter and how she feels about her parents. This would put the reasons for taking any action in proper perspective and build the necessary confidence with the parents and the child. He would object to the paternalistic attitude of the counselors and administrators towards the parents. He would certainly object to imputing that the parents are pursuing a stereotyped motive or reason for pushing their daughter and over-estimating her abilities.

Rawls would urge the counselors and administrators to empathize with the parents and their daughter trying to understand the merit of the parent's request because he maintains that our ability to create a just and fair society is tied directly to how fully we empathize with others, especially with the least fortunate. He would defend the most vulnerable in the situation – the child. If the transfer to another class would not increase the inequality of the other students, Rawls would not object to the move. Probably, he would invite the parents and the child to an open and frank discussion about the merits of the move.

Nel Nodding would recommend that the counselors and administrators, first of all, pay close attention to the relationship between the parents and their daughter. She would want to determine whether there is a positive reciprocal relationship between them. Do they trust each other? Are they pursuing a common goal? Do they listen to each other? The relationship between the parents, as the one-caring, and the child as the one-cared-for is of primary importance to Nodding for any successful decision. Furthermore, Nodding would insist on the child meeting with her current teacher and the teacher of the class where she might be move to. This would address the natural relationship (parent-child relationship) and the ethical relationship (teacher-child relationship). Only then could the path to a rational discussion of the move truly open because the caring relationship necessary for resolving problems has been met.

Carol Gilligan would first determine whether there is a caring relationship between the parents and the child. Only then would she invite everyone to participate in discussing the merits and demerits of the move. Probably, she would monitor the feeling and thoughts of the mother and the child because, she maintains they are too often neglected in any discussion about what is the right thing to do. She would view the paternalistic attitude of the counselors and administrators as an interference in building a mutually caring relationship. Imputing that the parents are pushing for advancing their child to the next grade because she is bright would be seen as a block to building a supportive relationship. Only after a mutual caring relationship had been established would she welcome any discussions about reasons for taking any action. Thus, she would try to maintain a positive dialogue about fairness and caring.

The common feature shared by the philosophers and psychologist is the need to pay primary attention to the feeling or sentiment of all parties involved. Hume stressed the central importance of the sentiment of humanity (fellow feeling) to serve as a basis for any discussion about the move. Nodding would insist that both, the parents and the counselors and administrators, should proceed from a caring relationship to ensure they are making the right decision about the move. Rawls would focus on the need to empathize with others especially with the most disadvantaged, the child. The parents should make sure that their daughter is comfortable with the move. Gilligan would pay close attention to the mutual caring relationship especially between the mother and her daughter.

Recent studies in neuroscience[112] offer a challenging perspective on the relationship between cognition and the affect. Antonio Damasio, for example, identified the crucial role emotions play in structuring human thought. As part of his research he studied the effects that damage to parts of the brain can have on human behavior and decision-making. For example, one of his patients suffered from a neurological disease that damaged part of his brain. In spite of the damage the patient was articulate, retained his memory, performed calculations and mastered abstract problems, but the patient had no sense of feelings - no sense of empathy. The damage occurred in that part of the brain that allows a person to experience feeling – the person had no sense of feeling - no sense of empathy; hence no sense of moral concern. Damagio concluded that "certain aspects of the process of emotion and feeling are indispensable for rationality[113]."

Neurologists have observed bizarre behaviors related to feelings, emotions and thinking in some brain damaged patients such as stroke victims who seem unable to express sadness, anxiety, anger or fear. Consequently, they are unable to make sound judgments. These observations have led neuroscientists to focus on that part of the brain where emotions and thinking interact, the anterior cingulate cortex which Damagio described as follows:

> The damage to this sector not only produces impairment in movement, emotion, and attentiveness, but also causes a virtual suspension of the animation of

action and of thought process such that reason is no longer viable[114].

Rifkin concludes that neuroscientists maintain that "the act of thinking combines sensations, feelings, emotions, and abstract thinking in an embodied way[115]."

Brooks responds to this question in a holistic way in *The Road to Character* by providing a gripping account of the journeys travelled by famous people including Francis Perkins, Ida Eisenhower, Dorothy Day, George Marshal, Philip Randolf, George Elliot (Mary Ann), St. Augustine and Samuel Johnson. Brooks observes that "each [had] the power to confront [his or her] weakness, tackle [his or her] sins, and that in the course of this confrontation, [he/she] built character[116]." For Brooks, character combines sensations, feelings, emotions, and abstract thinking.

It is one thing to maintain that a sense of empathy underlies moral reasoning; but it's quite another matter to know how to attend to it as a conscious priority for engaging in moral reasoning. That is why I acknowledge the importance of empathy as well as moral reasoning. The next chapter describes how moral values principle tests can prompt people to be empathic as they think through moral dilemmas to resolve them in a just and fair manner.

Chapter 11
Moral Values Principle Tests

Earlier I mentioned Kahneman[118] who addressed the challenge of deep thinking which he called level 2 thinking or slow thinking. Frequently there is no time to engage in deep thinking in the midst of a moral dilemma. That's why Kahneman recommends that people take time to reflect on difficult moral dilemmas when they are not in the midst of a crisis and have time to think through hypothetical situations which require deep thinking. That can prepare people to engage in what Kahneman calls fast thinking or intuitive thinking in a moment of crisis.

To that end, I introduce moral values principle tests developed by Kurt Baier in *A Moral Point of View*[117] because they can challenge us to consider others or empathize with them as we engage thoughtfully in resolving moral dilemmas. Briefly, here are the four Tests:

New Cases Test - consider the acceptability of a tentative value decision in similar new cases.

Role Exchange Test - encourage people to apply a value decision to themselves before prescribing it for others.

Subsumption Test - explore the interrelationship of principles by prioritizing competing principles.

Universal Consequences Test - consider the consequences of applying a decision to all like hypothetical or real situations. (Figure 11)

```
MORAL VALUES PRINCIPLE TESTS
1. Role Exchange
2. New Cases
3. Subsumption
4. Universal Consequences
```

Figure 11: Moral Values Principle Tests

Here is a more detailed introduction to the four moral values principle tests and the dissonance they generate.

New Cases Test

By applying the New Cases Test, people can consider whether the value decision made in one case also applies to a similar new case. If a decision made in one case also applies to another similar case, that might confirm a decision. If a decision applies to multiple similar cases that might add even more confidence in a decision. Applying the New Cases Test does not guarantee that a decision was right, but it might help to confirm a decision.

Let's revisit the story of the French soccer Captain, Thierry Henry (see Chapter 8), who remained silent about his handling a ball that led to the game-tying goal that gave France a spot in the World Cup. Did Thierry do the morally right thing in remaining silent when the referee did not call him on the foul play? Many people, including Irish fans, their Prime Minister and French gym teachers, did not think so. One way to resolve this issue is to ask whether we should coach children, say 12 year old soccer players, to hide bad plays that referees have missed. Is that how we want to teach children how to play fair? In other words, we would be applying the issue of what constitutes fair play to a new case, 12 year old soccer players. This enables us to look at the issue of *fairness* from the perspective of two similar cases.

Here is another example. Suppose in a discussion about the voting age in federal elections, Joe asserts that lowering the voting age is bad because people under the age of eighteen are politically immature. His friend, Sally, might challenge Joe's view by shifting the discussion to a comparison of the political maturity of stock brokers and eighteen year old high school students. In other words, can it be established that stock brokers possess more political maturity than eighteen year old high school students? If the answer is no, then the political maturity of eighteen year olds might not be an acceptable basis for denying them the right to vote. On the other hand, if the answer is yes, that stock brokers possess more political maturity than eighteen year old high school students, their immaturity might be considered as a necessary though not sufficient basis for denying eighteen years olds the right to vote. Applying the issue of political maturity to a new case might help to resolve the issue of expanding the voting age.

Role Exchange Test

I mentioned earlier that due to the emotional component in making value decisions, people sometimes prescribe action for other people which they would find entirely unacceptable for themselves. That's why it may be important to apply the role exchange test to determine the fairness of a decision. Suppose Don's neighbour, Peter, argued that no able-bodied man should receive welfare allowance for himself or his family. Don might ask Peter to consider the following situation. Suppose you were a technician at the James Bay Power Development plant in Canada and you were laid off for a whole year due to damages caused by a fire at the plant. Since you were laid off in the middle of winter along with 900 other men working at the same plant, you fail to get another job for months. Should your family go hungry just because you were laid off due to no fault of your own along with 900 other workers at a time of the year when few new jobs were available? At this point Peter might be ready to qualify his statement. He might even concede that there might be some circumstantial situations where an able-bodied person might be in need of welfare allowance and should receive it. When Peter put himself in the situation described by Don, he applied the role exchange test which might persuade him to reconsider his viewpoint. He imagined himself being unemployed and unable to find a job necessary to maintain his payments.

Subsumption Test

This test invites people to explore the interrelationship of principles such as the value of the life of a person verses the value of inanimate objects such as property. When there is strong disagreement about a value decision due to disagreement over the applicability of principles, it might be necessary to prioritize them. I am reminded of the sinking boat story. Here is my version of it.

Three men, David age 19, Tom age 39 with a family of two children, and Peter age 81 went fishing on an unfamiliar lake. They brought with them Peter's dog, a bag of dog food, a box of sandwiches and $1250.00 worth of fishing gear. The men agreed to allow Tom to bring his 10 year old son as well.

As they were fishing on an unfamiliar lake, they scraped the bottom of the boat on some sharp rocks causing the boat to spring a leak. Frantically, they headed for the nearest shore. However, they soon realized that they would have to lighten the load to get back to shore safely. So what should they throw over-board? What's more valuable – the 12 year old boy, the fishing gear, the dog, the 81 year old man, etc? You get the picture – they would have to prioritize and that's not going to be easy. Initially the decision was fairly easy – throw out the dog food, the fishing gear and the sandwiches. When that proved to be insufficient, they faced difficult questions, 'What goes over-board next – the dog or the young boy or possibly one of the men? If one of the men, which one based on what criteria – age, strength, family, etc?

The people in the boat would have to apply the subsumption test. They would have to consider the value of life versus the value of inanimate objects such as the dog food and the fishing gear. It got much more difficult when they had to prioritize the value of the life of a young boy versus the life of an old man or any of the men. First, they had to apply the principle of the value of human life verses the value of things. That was relatively easy – the value of a human being is greater than the value of things such as the dog food or fishing gear. Next they had to prioritize the principle of life of an old person verses the life of a young person. Unfortunately, applying the subsumptin test did not help them with this moral dilemma which goes to show that a particular test may not always help to resolve moral dilemmas.

Universal Consequences Test

Suppose teacher A punished a fifteen year old boy for denying that he had stolen teacher B's car keys when in fact, he had stolen them. In other words, teacher A punished the boy for lying and not for what the boy may have intended to do with the keys. Suppose Teacher B agrees with Teacher A that the boy should be punished but disagrees with Teacher A's reason for punishing the boy. Teacher B thinks that the boy should be punished because stealing people's car keys probably increases the temptation to steal cars. In short, teacher A maintains the boy should be punished for *lying* and teacher B insists that the boy should be punished because of the possible consequences of his action, namely, increasing car theft.

Neither teacher is willing to give in to the other teacher's argument. Finally, in desperation Teacher B asks Teacher A to consider the consequences of punishing everyone for telling lies or making false statements. What about the problem of selective perception frequently characterizing witnesses at the scene of an accident? What about a teacher who signs in a fellow teacher who is late for school? What about failing to report some personal income on the income tax returns? What about the white lie to cover a minor breach of rules in order to avoid embarrassment? What about a *white lie* to get a friend off the hook? What about a lie to protect the innocent in time of war? These are just a few questions Teacher B might ask Teacher A to challenge him to consider the universal consequences of punishing people whenever they make false statements. In other words, Teacher B is asking Teacher A to apply the Universal Consequences Test to reconsider his justification for punishing the boy for lying.

The moral values principle tests are not designed to resolve issues (guarantee right answers) but to justify a moral decision. As I showed in the scenarios above, the tests sometimes can help to generate the empathy necessary to resolve moral dilemmas. For example, when Peter argued that no able-bodied man should receive welfare allowance for himself or his family, Don challenged Peter's view of what is the right thing to do by presenting a scenario where a family man lost his job. In other words, Don questioned Peter's view of one of the categories of the Principled Thinking Model, *rights*. Second he invited Peter to feel a sense of empathy for the family man who lost his job by putting himself into the situation of that family man – hypothetically doing a role exchange. This might persuade Peter to re-consider his original position by acknowledging that there are situations where an able-bodied man should receive welfare allowance.

Why is it important to demand that people justify their positions? Don's hypothetical scenario speaks to this question. Imagine the hardship created for families when enough people in a community or country would take the original position taken by Peter, namely, no able-bodied man should receive welfare allowance. That could create unjust hardship for many families due to no fault of their own.

Once again, there is no assurance that the application of the moral values principle tests will help to resolve moral dilemmas by challenging people to be empathic. The tests can, in fact, stimulate different kinds of dissonance – logical, cultural, experiential, and moral. When people experience dissonance, they try to resolve or reduce it. Sometimes dissonance may actually interfere with resolving moral dilemmas. Consider the following account of different kinds of dissonance and how they might affect people's ability to make moral decisions.

Chapter 12
Dissonance

We are indebted to Leon Festinger[119] for a better understanding of dissonance. Dissonance, according to Festinger, is psychologically uncomfortable and therefore motivates people to try to reduce it by resolving the dilemma which created the dissonance or by to trying to avoid it. In fact, dissonance can result in increased anxiety, fear, etc. Here are four types of dissonance Festinger has identified which I have applied to different scenarios.

Logical dissonance

Dissonance can be generated by logical inconsistency. This can be initiated by replacing a positive statement with a negative statement. For example, note the replacement of the statement *will attend* with *will not attend* in the following scenario.

Sally was looking forward to the final basketball game of the season in which she had played exceptionally well. She hoped that her dad would take time to see her play in this final game even though he had failed to show up at any of the games throughout the season. Every time she had a game, he insisted he could not show up because he had to attend one of his many business meetings. This time however, he promised to come to the game and root for her. Once more, Sally hoped her dad would come. The day before the all-important game, she received a text message from her dad expressing his regret that he would not be able to show up at the final game – an emergency meeting had been scheduled which he must attend. Sadly, Sally's worst fears had come true – a *yes* had become a *no*. *Disappointment* does not capture her feeling of dissonance. How could *yes* mean *no*? How could her dad *make a promise* and *break the promise*? To Sally, that felt like a violation of the principle of *keeping a promise*. She did not know what to do to reduce the dissonance she felt about her dad breaking his promise.

Cultural dissonance

A clash of cultural mores can generate dissonance which prompts people to make an effort to reduce the uncomfortable feeling of incongruity between conflicting cultural mores or customs. Read this modified story about the residents of Grand Forks who experienced a flood of the century. They experienced cultural dissonance when they heard about the results of Dr. Anderson's second study which came to a different conclusion than her first study.

A flood of the century had inundated the entire city of Grand Forks causing the downtown to be destroyed by water and fire. As for their homes, many had been damaged beyond repair. Dr. Anderson had been contracted to determine the effects of the flood on the residents. Her study showed that everything changed dramatically two years after the flood. Comparing two years after the flood with two years prior showed a 6 percent increase in hospital admissions and a 14 percent increase in visits to a clinic. The two years after the flood also saw a substantial increase in the divorce rate. The residents felt certain that the change in their health was directly related to the flood.

Suppose Dr. Anderson concluded in a follow-up study that the change in the social and personal well-being of many of the residents of Grand Forks was due to a radical change in the diet of the residents. Suppose further, the second study showed that in the time of stress after the Flood, the residents developed a habit of eating comfort foods, such as candies, and eating between meals which resulted in an increase in illnesses such as diabetes. This new information would have created more emotional stress and confusion for the residents because it suggested that they were somewhat responsible for their personal and social well-being. Dr. Anderson's follow-up study would have created a significant level of cultural dissonance for the residents which they would not or could not appreciate. Dr. Anderson's view of the impact of eating *junk food* clashed with the residents' view of what caused the increased illnesses after the flood.

The residents might have reduced the dissonance created by the second study conducted by Dr. Anderson by simply ignoring the results of the second study. Festinger[120] points out that sometimes people reduce their dissonant feeling by walking away from the cause of their dissonant feeling.

Experiential dissonance

A person can experience dissonance when past experiences do not align with current experiences or when two similar events seem to result in very different experiences. In the following scenario, David could not understand how a flood could affect people in Grand Forks so differently from his own experience. That caused David to experience experiential dissonance.

Suppose a graduate student, David, read Dr. Anderson's report and drew his own conclusion based on his personal experience with a flood he experienced years ago in another city. David and his family had not experienced any unusual illness in the years after their flood. So, how could the personal well-being of the residents of Grand Forks be affected by the Flood of the Century? Reading about the experience of the residence of Grand Forks created an experiential dissonance for David. It was confusing and frustrating for him.

David had no way of reducing the dissonance he experienced due to the clash of his personal experience with what the residents of Grand Forks experienced.

Cognitive dissonance

According to Festinger[121], cognitive dissonance refers to situations where two cognitive elements do not fit together; they may be inconsistent or contradictory. For example, suppose John Doe knew that there were only friends at his birthday party but he still felt afraid, he would be caught between two cognitive elements – friends and fear – that do not make any sense together. Cognitive dissonance creates a feeling of discomfort which drives people to attempt to avoid it or resolve it. The following scenario illustrates the cognitive dissonance experienced by a city council and their attempt to resolve it.

Suppose the City Council of Grand Forks debated the implications of not taking the necessary action to prevent another devastating flood. In addition to the apparent effects of the flood identified by Dr. Anderson, many other obvious consequences were identified by them including loss of property, loss of homes, and loss of jobs just to mention a few. Hence, the government faced a moral dilemma. Should they spend enormous funds, which the city did not have, to protect the city from another flood of the century? Or should they do nothing and not run up a deficit. Should they take a chance that a devastating flood will not occur for at least another century or longer? City Council was faced with the question, 'What is the right thing to do?' This posed a moral dilemma causing cognitive dissonance for the Council. The cognitive dissonance was created for the City Council by the clash of two elements: incur a huge debt to protect the city from future floods OR avoid huge debts by doing nothing to protect the city from another flood of the century. They chose the former.

The moral values principle tests can cause various kinds of dissonance which may or may not help to resolve moral dilemmas. Leon Festinger[122], social psychologist best known for his work on cognitive dissonance, suggests that dissonance generated through applying a cognitive process might offer the most promising approach to reducing dissonance. He identified several procedures used by people to reduce cognitive dissonance even though he acknowledges that these are tentative suggestions[123]. First, sometimes people alter or discard some of the elements that are creating the dissonance. For example, Sally could have tried to ignore that her dad had broken his promise. But, she couldn't. Second, some people focus on the consonant elements and add more consonant elements. For example, David could have searched for more evidence to explain why the health of the residents of Grand Forks deteriorated after the flood. Third, sometimes people make every effort to selectively *forget* the elements which cause dissonance. The residents of Grand Forks simply denied the importance of a healthy diet. That way they need not assume any responsibility for their reduced health after the flood. In contrast, city Council faced the cognitive dissonance and decided to address the challenge head on.

This brief review of several moral values principle tests and the kinds of dissonance they generate present possible pathways to address the emotional aspect of resolving moral dilemmas. That pathway is to apply the moral values principle tests with the hope that they will generate cognitive dissonance as opposed to the other forms of dissonance.

Part III

Application of the Principled Thinking Model and the Moral Values Principle Tests

Before we look at how the Principled Thinking Model coupled with the Moral Values Principle Tests can be used to resolve moral dilemmas, let's review what got us to this point. I start the book with several dilemmas which required solving conflict situations. Remember Tommy who was asked by his Grandma to share some of his pennies with his brother Billy but refused to do it; Jack and Peter were asked by their principal to agree on appropriate punishment for Peter who had kicked Jack in the head. Both involved moral dilemmas which required resolving the rights and responsibilities of the parties involved in a conflict. Since my goal for the book is to show how conflicts can be resolved by thinking through moral dilemmas, I introduced some of the research supporting my goal by referring to the works of Jean Piaget, Lawrence Kohlberg, and Daniel Kahneman. Then I proceeded to present the categories and concepts of the Principled Thinking Model for thinking through moral dilemmas in pursuit of justice. That's where I introduced two hypothetical teach-ers, Mae and Bill, who engage in conversations using the categories of the Principled Thinking Model. The conversation demonstrates how the categories might be used in every day conversation. Through those conversations, Mae concluded that thinking through moral dilemmas is inadequate for resolving moral dilemmas. She maintains that a sense of empathy or fellow feeling is essential to resolve them. Bill appreciated Mae's insight and refers to it as an Eureka moment.

That led me to explore what philosophers, David Hume, John Rawls, and Nel Nodding as well as psychologist Carol Gilligan, had to say about the role of empathy in resolving moral dilemmas or conflicts. I described how the emotional aspect, empathy, can serve as a basis for resolving moral dilemmas. That's when I introduced Kurt Baier's Moral Values Principle Tests that may help to reduce the dissonance generated by the conflict inherent in moral dilemmas.

That leaves me with the challenge of showing how the Principled Thinking Model and the Moral Values Principle Tests together can be used to address the conflict inherent in moral dilemmas. To that end, I applied them to the following nine scenarios and reports.

Censoring Internet Access
Irate Parent
Considerate parent
Arthur's Moral Dilemma
Cyber Bullying
Civil Society and Faith-based Communities
International Duties or Responsibilities
The Enemy Is Neglect of Mental Illness
Reconciliation

These scenarios and reports demonstrate how thinking and a sense of empathy were and were not applied to resolve moral dilemmas in pursuit of justice or fairness. This is apparent in the failure to resolve the dissonance in *The Irate Parent* where the parent appealed only to her daughter's rights and the principal's obligations. The parent showed no empathy for the parties caught in the moral dilemma of considering the rights and obligations of all parties, including the teacher. In contrast, both, thinking and a sense of empathy are evident in Arthur's determination to resolve a moral dilemma in *Arthur's Moral Dilemma*.

Chapter 13
Censoring Internet Access

A reporter requested to interview me when I was an assistant superintendent of a school division to discuss the issue of censorship. She was referring to our practice of limiting student access to high speed Internet access in the high schools. When high schools first introduced high speed Internet in schools in the 1990's, some parents and educators raised serious concerns about the issue of giving adolescents un-restricted access to the Internet. Should young people have unfettered access to whatever is available online? If not, what constraints are appropriate and why? People held strong views on both sides of this issue. Some feared that young people might access inappropriate content online in class. Others saw the Internet as an opportunity for young people to explore the universe from the safety of the classroom. The issue came to a head when a few of our high school students contacted several news outlets to complain about restricting students' access to the Internet in high school. This led to the following interview with a reporter as I recall it.

> "Good Morning Dr. Otto, my name is Ms. Jain (not the reporter's real name) and I am calling from Radio CDK. One of the high school students from your school division called me to complain about the policy of censoring student access to the Internet in her high school. I would like to discuss this with you. Are you available tomorrow morning at 8:00 in our studio?"

I assured her I was. As Assistant Superintendent for Curriculum, I was not surprised at the request since several reporters had already contacted me in my office to discuss the same issue. At the appointed time, I was escorted into the Studio for a live interview.

The reporter immediately cut to the chase by asking, "What are your reasons for censoring the use of the Internet in your high schools?"

I replied by asking a few simple questions.

"Is there a school close to where you live?"

She replied, "Yes."

"Does it have a library?"

Her answer of course was, "Yes."

"Can students and parents access any and all reading materials in the school library?"

She qualified her answer by saying, "Well, not really. The library focuses on acquiring appropriate learning resources based on the Curriculum."

I responded by saying, "The Internet in our high schools is an extension of the school library and access to the learning resources online should follow the same library guidelines for providing students with access to appropriate and quality learning resources."

Instantly, the mike went dead and the reporter muttered," I never thought about the Internet in those terms."

Politely, I was escorted out of the studio and offered the radio station's mug for showing up for the interview. I have treasured that mug to this day[124].

Let's see what Bill and Mae's response was years later to the assistant superintendent's recollection of the interview. Recall Mae and Bill are 9th grade teachers at Middletown Middle School. Mae has been teaching English for the past four years and Bill is a twelve year History teacher. Here is part of their discussion about the interview.

Conversation – Mae and Bill

"I must admit I was not impressed with the assistant supt.; what century did he come from?" objected Bill. "Doesn't he understand that there is no way you can control access to the Internet? Even the Chinese have tried and failed miserably!"

"Hold it a moment," retorted Mae. "You must remember that this interview took place in the '90s ... just when high speed Internet became available in schools! That's light years ago in terms of the Internet Age."

"I have to give credit to the reporter ... she politely asked the assistant supt. for reasons," observed Bill.

"What troubles me about the reporter," said Mae, "is she focussed only on the rights of students. Why didn't she challenge the assistant supt. on his responsibilities in censoring access to the Internet?"

"I'm surprised that the reporter did not think about the Internet as an extension of the school library ... an incredible extension giving students access to a world-wide library!" exclaimed Bill.

"What I found really bizarre is that the assistant supt. did not include students in a discussion of appropriate use of the Internet. This could have been done so easily at each high school led by the teachers," insisted Mae. "I wonder what motivated him not to insist on this course of action."

"I agree with you," added Bill. "That kind of discussions could have led to a fair policy of using the Internet which students could understand and accept."

"It could have led to a policy which would have given students what they deserved ... access to a world-wide library!" added Mae.

"What's more, the reporter could have challenged the assistant supt. by asking a few tough questions," asserted Bill. "She could have asked him how he would have felt if his son needed to conduct a specific search which required access to the Internet but was denied access to high speed Internet at his high school."

"Or," Mae chimed in," the reporter could have asked, "What if you had been denied access to some of the books and articles in the library you needed when you were in high school?"

To which Bill added, "The reporter could have asked 'What if the government would deny citizens access to information at its discretion? Is that the kind of government you want?"

I like your questions about the universal consequences of censorship," said Mae. "I think it would have put the assistant supt. in an impossible situation defending his decision."

"I get your point" responded Bill. "She could have asked a really difficult question about what is more important in dealing with this issue: blocking access to specific information on the Internet or coaching students on the responsible use of access to information on the Internet."

More to himself, Bill mused, "The reporter could have had a great interview with the assistant supt. if she had asked these questions. What's more it could have served as a great lesson in responsible access to information on the Internet."

The following Chart (Figure 12) identifies the issues related to the Principled Thinking Model which the reporter pursued and the issues she did not pursue. If the reporter had considered all five categories, she could have continued with the interview. The conversation between Mae and Bill suggests how the conversation could have proceeded to shed light on the controversial issue of providing youth with access to the Internet.

PRINCIPLED THINKING MODEL	SCENARIO: Censoring Internet Access	
	Reporter did not consider	**Reporter considered**
Duty	She did not consider the School Division's responsibilities to provide students with the best learning resources.	
Rights		She focused only on students' rights.
Motive	She did not attempt to determine the assistant superintendent's motive for limiting students' access to the Internet.	
Desert	She did not explore what students deserve.	
Just	She did not explore how justice or fairness could be applied in this situation.	

Figure 12: Principled Thinking Model applied to Censoring the Internet

The following Chart (Figure 13) identifies the moral values principle tests which the reporter could have applied to the assistant superintendent's decision.

MORALS VALUES PRINCIPLE TESTS	SCENARIO: Censoring Internet Access Questions the reporter could have asked.
New Cases Test	What if your son needed to conduct a specific Internet search but was denied access to the Internet in his high school?
Role Exchange Test	What if you had been denied access to some of the books and articles in the school library when you were in high school?
Subsumption Test	What is more important – blocking access to specific information on the Internet or coaching students on responsible access to information on the Internet?
Universal Consequences Test	What if the government would deny access to information at its discretion?

Figure 13: Moral Values Principle Tests applied to Censoring Internet Access

These questions suggested by Mae and Bill, which were never asked, could have elicited a sense of empathy from the principal towards the students' predicament when their access to the Internet was restricted. The appeal to the assistant supt.'s own son's need to conduct his research on the Internet, the principal's dependence on access to books, and citizen's right to access information denied by their government bring the issue of *access* close to the assistant supt. Challenging him to prioritize two competing principles could have created sufficient cognitive dissonance to urge him to reconsider his original decision to restrict students' access to the Internet. He might have decided to open a process of consultation with parents and students before introducing restricted access to the Internet.

Chapter 14
Irate Parent

In this Scenario, a parent, Mr. Brown, is convinced that the novel, *Of Mice and Men*, should not be used in his daughter's high school class. Notice how the parent approached this issue with the principal.

Mr. Brown, an irate parent, burst into the principal's office and dove into his objections, "Why do you permit your English teacher to insist that her class read *Of Mice and Men* by John Steinbeck ... (he paused for a moment to catch his breath) ... when you know the book is not on the required reading list of the State Education Ministry? That's wrong," he went on to say before the principal could say a word, "It's morally wrong! I find the language used in that book utterly offensive ... all that cursing! I repeat," he stressed, "that is morally wrong. You have a responsibility to remove that book from the school curriculum immediately!"

"What's more, it is wrong to require my daughter to read a novel which is offensive to me whether she agrees with me or not", he asserted.

All the while, the principal was wondering how she might respond as she listened to Mr. Brown. Even though she suspected that the parent's motives were somewhat self-serving, she respected his moral indignation. She agreed that it would not be wrong to offer his daughter an option to study an alternative novel.

However, the principal felt she should not ignore the way Mr. Brown had verbally accosted her. Hence, she said to him, "I will review the situation with my staff at the next Department meeting in two weeks time. In the meantime, your daughter is required to stay in the class where *Of Mice and Men* is studied."

She considered this action to be an appropriate way of expressing her disapproval of the Mr. Brown's action because she felt the he deserved this response. Never-the-less, she viewed him as a just person because she agreed that the action he demanded was the right action for his daughter. At the same time, she was troubled at the thought of requiring the English teacher to individu-alize the English course to meet the demands of any and all parents. How could the English teacher teach such a customized course? This raised another perplexing issue – should she prioritize the demands of the parent, the teacher's workload or the needs of the students? This posed a difficult moral dilemma for her[125].

Conversation – Mae and Bill

"ARGHHH! The parent sure laced into the principal!" exclaimed Mae. "He made it absolutely clear that the principal had a duty to remove the offensive novel from the school immediately."

"I think he went a step too far when he insisted that it is wrong to require his daughter to read a novel which is offensive to him whether his daugh-ter agrees with him or not. This suggested that his daughter's view really did not matter," observed Bill.

"What's more, Mr. Brown maintained that this was a moral issue of right and wrong. But, is that the way to treat your daughter?" Mae wondered.

"I'm OK with the parent defending his daughter's rights," insisted Bill, "but is he really defending her rights when he adds whether she agrees with me or not? Or is he defending his own rights?"

"Why is Mr. Brown so angry?" asked Mae. "Is that the way to deal with what he regards as a moral issue?"

"Honestly," said Bill, "people can feel strongly when they sense a violation of their rights."

"I guess so," murmured Mae. "It makes me wonder what really motivated Mr. Brown."

"I agree with you. What really troubles me," said Bill, "is the parent's motive. His proposed action about removing the novel from the curriculum seems to be more about himself than about the rights of his daughter. That does not seem to me a morally good motive; it seems self-serving. His proposed action was not wrong but I question his motive."

Mae agreed but added, "Although I suspect that the parent's motives were somewhat self-serving, I accept the parent's moral indignation. I agree that it would not be wrong to offer his daughter the option to study an alternative novel."

"But," added Bill, "did the principal act from a morally good motive? Was she prejudiced against Mr. Brown, who verbally accosted her? If so, her action would not be morally good either."

"Of course," insisted Mae, "that puts into question the principal's decision to express a mild form of disapproval by delaying her decision; she probably felt the parent deserved it. She probably could not resist her spontaneous attitude of disapproval. At the same time, she chose what form her feeling of disapproval should take."

"She certainly did not think the parent deserved to be punished," observed Bill.

"At the same time," Mae felt, "the principal viewed Mr. Brown as a just person because the action he demanded might be the right action for his daughter. The principal was committed to being fair with the parent even though he had been irate about the use of the novel in the local high school."

"I am not so quick to assume that the parent was acting from a morally good motive," insisted Bill. "I suspect that he acted more out of self interest which is not a morally good motive."

"I was impressed with the way the principal made her decision," said Mae. "She was concerned about the workload for the teacher who would be expected to individualize the English course to meet the demand of one parent."

"And," added Bill, "the principal struggled with the challenge of having to prioritize the needs of parents, teachers, and students. Which of these should be her top priority?"

The following Chart (Figure 14) shows how the Principled Thinking Model was applied differently by the parent and the principal.

PRINCIPLED THINKING MODEL	SCENARIO: Irate Parent	
	Irate Parent	Principal
Duty	The principal has a duty: "You have a responsibility to remove that book from the school curriculum immediately!"	The principal felt she should not ignore the way the parent had verbally accosted her.

Rights	my daughter has a right to study an alternative novel	The principal recognized the student's right to read an alternative novel
Motive		The principal felt that the parent's motives were somewhat self-serving
Desert		The principal felt that the parent deserved this response.
Just		The principal viewed the parent as a just person.

Figure 14: Principled Thinking Model applied to Irate Parent

The contrast between the approach used by the parent and the principal was striking. The principal considered all aspects of the model whereas the irate parent considered only two – duties and rights (Figure 14). It was exceedingly difficult for the principal to resolve the dilemma or conflict in a just and fair way since the parent dealt only with the duty of the principal and the rights of his daughter. The principal tried to explore all categories of the Principled Thinking Model but to no avail. This made it impossible for the two of them to resolve the dilemma – the conflict remained.

The following Chart (Figure 15) shows which moral values principle tests the principal applied.

MORAL VALUES PRINCIPLE TESTS	SCENARIO: Irate Parent Tests the Principal applied
New Cases Test	

Role Exchange Test	
Subsumption Test	Should she prioritize the demands of parents or the teacher's workload? Maybe she should focus on the needs of students.
Universal Consequences Test	- The principal was troubled at the thought of requiring the English teacher to individualize the English course to meet the demand of every parent. - Should she require it of all teachers?

Figure 15: Moral Values Principle Tests applied to Irate Parent

The parent did not apply any tests. The principal was left on her own to deal with the emotional aspect of the conflict about what to expect from teachers. She showed that she was sensitive to the workload of her teachers by applying two tests: Subsumption Test (Should she prioritize the demands of the parents or the teacher's workload? Maybe she should focus on the needs of students) and Universal Consequences Test (The principal was troubled at the thought of requiring the English teacher to individualize the English course to meet the demand of every parent. Should she require it of all teachers?). Since the parent did not consider the dilemma his request created for the principal and the teacher, the two of them could not resolve the dilemma. This raises the question: What might the principal have done to engage the parent in considering both sides of the problem of removing the novel from the school? In other words, what might have initiated the cognitive dissonance for the parent to reconsider his position? Suppose the principal had asked the parent about other books which, in his (parent's) opinion should be removed? Or, what if the principal had asked the parent whether all parents should be free to remove any book they object to? Might a discussion of these hypothetical new cases have opened a conversation about what to do about censoring books used in schools?

I repeat that it is important to emphasize that the moral values principle tests do not resolve issues (guarantee right answers) but serve as an attempt to justify decisions of right and wrong.

Chapter 15
Considerate Parent

Notice how differently Mrs. Jones approached the principal of her daughter's school which also allowed the use of the novel, *Of Mice and Men*.

Mrs. Jones, whose daughter attended another high school, was anxious about what to say to the principal, Mr. Anderson, about her objection to the use of John Steinbeck's novel, *Of Mice and Men* in English class. Young people hear enough foul language on the street and in public places. Moreover, she felt she had a duty to raise her objections because she has a right to defend her daughter's rights – her right to read an alternative novel which does did not contain offensive language. She simply had to make her case, first to the principal and if the principal failed to act on her objection, then to the School Board. Mrs. Jones really wanted to do what is right ... her motives were noble. That's why she kept thinking about what she should say to the principal.

When she asked her husband for his opinion, he replied with a few questions, Did our daughter object to the language used in Steinbeck's novel or do you object to it? Should she have a right to object to the use of the novel in class or should we, as her parents, have that right? What if she trusts the way her teacher uses the novel to challenge students to understand different types of literature?

Mrs. Jones felt that her husband had raised some very good questions. Am I defending my rights or the rights of our daughter? Have I asked my daughter how she feels about the use of Steinbeck's novel in class Does she trust her teacher in the way he uses the novel in class? Now these questions are racing through her mind because she wants to do what is right for her daughter.

She was determined to present her concerns with respect. Putting herself in the principal's place, she was certain that the principal did not do wrong for wrong's sake. This is no time to be critical of him personally ... he did not deserve that.

Why was the principal condoning the use of this novel, she wondered. Maybe the teacher randomly assigned Steinbeck's novel to her daughter's class. That might be wrong, but not necessarily unjust. On the other hand, if the teacher had picked her daughter's class for some reason to read a novel containing foul language that could be discriminatory.

She picked up the phone to make an appointment with the principal. Justice had to be done. Her daughter's rights had to be respected[126].

Conversation – Bill and Mae

"How refreshing to read about Mrs. Jones' approach to dealing with her objection to the use of John Steinbeck's novel, *Of Mice and Men*, in her daughter's class," observed Mae. "It was so different from Mr. Brown's angry reaction."

"Agreed, but Mrs. Jones did not leave the principal off the hook either," insisted Bill. "She focused on the principal's duty just as Mr. Brown did."

"And on her daughter's rights," added Mae.

"Come to think of it," maintained Bill, "Mrs. Jones also asserted her own right to raise the issue. She maintained it was her right to raise her objection to the use the novel in her daughter's class."

"I think Mrs. Jones is a very sensitive person," observed Mae. "She was very concerned about her own motive for approaching the principal about the use of the novel in class ... she really wanted to do what is right for her daughter. Acting from a morally good motive was important to her. What really impressed me was her effort to understand the principal; she put herself in his shoes," added Mae.

"She felt this is not the time to be critical of him personally," added Bill. "He did not do wrong for wrong's sake by permitting the teacher to use the novel in class."

"I think if Mrs. Jones had felt that if the principal had discriminated against her daughter," insisted Mae, "she would have planned to express stronger disapproval. But, she didn't believe for a moment that the principal discriminated against her daughter."

"I thought Mrs. Jones' husband asked questions which were right on the mark," insisted Bill. "Did our daughter object to the language used in Steinbach's novel or do you object to it? Should she have a right to object to the use of the novel in class or should we, as her parents, have that right? What if she trusts the way her teacher uses the novel to reflect certain types of literature? What's wrong with these questions?"

"I thought her husband was imputing a personal motive when he asked, 'Should she have a right to object to the use of the novel in class or should we, as her parents, have that right?' I certainly don't think that was helpful," insisted Mae.

Shifting the conversation back to the principal, Mae said, "I agree with Mrs. Jones that the principal did not act unjustly even though she believed that it was wrong to permit the use the novel in class because of the foul language in it."

"Let's compare, for a moment, the approach used by the two parents," suggested Bill. "Although, both parents arrived at the same conclusion, they did not think through the issues the same way."

"OK. Unlike the Irate Parent, Mrs. Jones considered the rights and duties of both, the principal and her daughter," observed Mae.

"The irate parent considered only his rights and the principal's duty," observed Bill.

"There is another big difference in the way the two parents approach this issue," added Mae. "The Irate parent seemed indifferent about the appropriateness of his action; he simply wanted to get the novel out of the school. Mrs. Jones, on the other hand, put herself in the shoes of the principal to get another perspective on the issue of removing the novel from the school curriculum."

"I agree with you. This step led her to the conclusion that the principal did not deserve to be criticized for his action. She was confident that he did not do wrong for wrong's sake," concluded Bill.

"At the same time," Mae reminded Bill, "Mrs. Jones was convinced that justice needed to be done."

To which Bill added, "I am impressed how Mrs. Jones thoughtfully reflected on determining the morally right course of action."

"We shouldn't overlook the principal's response to the irate parent," insisted Mae. "She used two ways of assessing the course of action she should take. She asked herself the question: "Should I prioritize the demands of the parent or the teacher's workload?" She followed up with the questions, "What might be the implications of making one exception for the daughter of the irate parent? Might teachers be expected to individualize their programs for any and all students in the future? Is that fair to teachers?"

"The principal felt the dilemma he faced," agreed Bill. "He had to prioritize the principles involved. That's never easy. What do you think he should do?"

"I was afraid you would ask," replied Mae. "I would have to think about it."

The following Chart (Figure 16) compares the use of the Principled Thinking Model by the two parents.

PRINCIPLED THINKING MODEL	SCENARIO: Irate Parent & Considerate Parent	
	Irate Parent	Considerate Parent
Duty	You have a responsibility to remove that book from the school curriculum immediately!	She (Mrs. Jones) had a duty to raise her objections
Rights	my daughter has a right to study an alternative novel	because she (Mrs. Jones) had a right to defend her daughter's rights
Motive		Mrs. Jones really wanted to do what is right ... her motives were noble
Desert		The principal did not deserve criticism
Just		justice needs to be done: respect her daughter's rights

Figure 16: Principled Thinking Model applied to Considerate Parent

In the previous chapter we saw how the irate parent dealt with the dilemma created by the principal when she permitted the English teacher to use a novel which contained offensive language. Mrs. Jones, the considerate parent, used a very different approach. She did what Kahneman[127] recommended when he suggests that people need to be engaged in *slow thinking* - deliberate and effortful thinking – before encountering a potentially difficult situation and not depend on *fast thinking* or intuitive thinking required in the moment of conflict. Mrs. Jones took time to reflect on what she should say to the principal before she met with him. This allowed her to think through the principal's responsibilities as well as her daughter's rights.

The use of the moral values principle tests in the two scenarios is compared in the following Chart (Figure 17).

MORAL VALUES PRINCIPLE TESTS	SCENARIO: Irate Parent & Considerate Parent		
	Irate Parent	Principal responding to the irate parent	Considerate Parent
New Cases Test			
Role Exchange Test			Putting herself in the principal's place
Subsumption Test		prioritize the demands of the parents, the teacher's workload, or the needs of the students.	

Universal Consequences Test		require the English teacher to individualize the English course to meet the demand of every parent.	

Figure 17: Moral Values Principle Tests applied to Irate Parent and Considerate Parent

Mrs. Jones wanted to do what is right; so she put herself in the principal's place; and she made sure she understood the difference between just and unjust acts before she picked up the phone to make an appointment. We don't know the results of her meeting with the principal, but based on Kahneman's advice about *slow thinking* she took the right steps to prepare herself for the meeting with the principal.

Chapter 16
Arthur's Moral Dilemma

This Chapter addresses the difficult decision a Church Board, under Arthur's leadership, had to make about the closure of their church while at the same time meeting the needs of the parishioners.

"I hope we made the right decision", muttered Arthur, Chairman of the Church Board, as he reflected on the most difficult decision his Board had made two hours ago. After 36 months of what seemed like never ending meetings, the Board had finally decided to recommend the closure of their church ... the revenue and membership simply did not justify keeping it open. The trend was clear. Over the past fifteen years, young and middle age people were not attending church in sufficient numbers to sustain it financially.

What troubled Arthur most was not the closure of their church as such, much as he deeply appreciated the spiritual and community service the church had offered for many decades. The traditional hymns, sermons and social events had served the regular parishioners very well for over 100 years. He anguished over the effect the closure would have on young and old who depended on the care they received from the church. His church had been a first responder to so many people suffering from illness, including mental illness.

In particular, he was thinking about sixty seven year old Emma (not her real name), who since her teenage years had suffered with mental illness. His church had been there when she needed support. Who would take care of her after the church is closed? Would she have the courage and confidence to transfer to another church in a nearby suburb? Would they attend to her needs the way his church had over the years? That seemed doubtful to him[128].

Conversation – Mae and Bill

"Just a caution," said Bill "I don't attend church, so I may not have much to say about this issue."

"That never stopped you before from speaking your mind," teased Mae. "Whether I agree with Arthur about the spiritual nourishment or the traditions of the church, I believe Arthur was sincere about wanting to do the right thing even if it included closing their church."

"I think he tried to assure himself that the Board had made the right decision. Maybe he was feeling some buyer's remorse which is quite common after a person has made a significant decision," suggested Bill.

"I think his anguish reflected more than that," insisted Mae."He was caught between his genuine desire to do what is right and a nostalgic feeling about what the church has meant to so many people, including himself. That's why he kept referring to sixty seven year old Emma."

"He raised an interesting point about Emma," acknowledged Bill. "I guess I never realized how churches serve communities especially people with complicated illnesses such as mental illness. Often, churches seem to be first responders. Arthur raised a good question when he asked who would support people like Emma after his church would be closed."

"May I ask you a difficult question?" asked Mae. "Does Emma have a right to appropriate care? I am referring not only to her legal rights but also her human rights even when it is not a legal right." Mae was on a roll. She continued, "Does she have a right to mental health services as a human being? Might Arthur's church have some obligations to protect Emma's human rights to receive support for her mental illness? Or, are her rights dependent on whether they are enshrined in law?"

"Here is how I see it," said Bill. "Arthur and the Board had a clear and convincing picture of the church's finances. The church could not be sustained on its current financial base. For that reason, it had to be closed. Hence, the Board decided to close it. So, what's the problem? The Board obviously had no choice."

"I'm surprised you don't get it," objected Mae to Bill's simplistic view of the issue. "Here is the dilemma. Arthur agreed with the Board that the church had to be closed because young and middle age people were not joining their church in sufficient numbers to sustain it. On the other hand, he felt a duty to continue to serve those who depend on the care they receive from the church. He felt the Board could not close the church doors and support those in need at the same time. This certainly felt like a conflict of responsibilities."

Bill was not about to take this lecture sitting down. So he retorted, "Surely Arthur realized that he had only a *prima facie* conflict of duties or an apparent conflict of duties. Since he could not perform both apparent duties, he would have to determine his actual duty."

"That's right," responded Mae with indignation. "I read in the local newspaper that Arthur reconvened the Board to present this moral dilemma, namely, to do what is the right thing for people like Emma." Before Bill could respond, she added, "The article went on to say that, after conducting extensive discussions once more, the Board decided not only to close the church but to build and support a community outreach centre in its place. That's quite a remarkable and ambitious decision!"

"WOW. That is remarkable," acknowledged Bill.

"Guess what Emma did," Mae recalled from the news article. "When she heard about the decision by the Church Board to establish a community outreach centre in her neighbourhood after the church would be closed, she wrote a thank you letter to Arthur. Want to see it? Here it is." Mae pulled the letter (Figure 18) from her purse to show it to Bill.

Dear Arthur,

Thank you for thinking about people like me ... we will have a place to get help after you close the church. Maybe you will offer some Sunday morning services and programs for us at the community centre as well.

How can I show my thanks to you and the Board? I hope someone will reward you for your thoughtfulness and generosity.

God bless you
Emma

Figure 18: Emma's letter

"And, do you want to know how the Board responded to the letter?" asked Mae. "To a person, they insisted they did not deserve Emma's kind words. They had simply done the right thing. They felt any sincere Board facing the problems they faced would have made the same decision. They certainly felt they had not gone beyond the call of duty in making their decisions."

"So what would the Board have had to do to go beyond the call of duty?" Bill asked out of curiosity.

Mae thought for a moment and replied, "Suppose the sale of the church would not have generated sufficient funds to build a community centre. If one or more of the Board members had decided to come up with the difference at considerable cost to themselves, they would have made an unusual financial commitment. That might be considered going beyond the call of duty."

Bill was being difficult. Reflecting his belief that all events are caused by something, he asked, "Do you really think the Board members exercised their free will in the decision to recommend to the congregation to close the church?"

Trying not to show her frustration with Bill when he was asking his favorite mischievous questions, she replied, "I think you are asking the question, 'Is the act of choosing determined or does it have a cause?'"

"That's the question," replied Bill. "And, if choosing is not caused it would be like a bolt from the blue. If that were so, how could a person be considered responsible for what he chooses? If choices are not caused by something, they would be inexplicable."

To which Mae responded, "Freedom of will seems to refer to choices determined by reasons rather than by causes."

"But," argued Bill, "reasons are just another set of causes!"

"I think," Mae added, "people generally assume that they can make judgments of right and wrong. This suggests that people have, to some degree, freedom of will."

Not knowing how to respond to Mae's common sense observation, Bill changed the subject by asking, "Was their decision just?"

"That depends," replied Mae. "Did they act with impartiality? Did they acknowledge the rights of the people affected by their decision? Did they give people what they deserve? How would you answer these questions as they relate to the Board's decision?" asked Mae.

"I find it significant," said Bill, "that, as they thought about their response to a dilemma, they considered its impact on a particular case, Emma, who suffered from mental illness and had received support from their church for many years. The Board's conclusion that a decision must not only be morally right but must also be just," is new to me," added Bill.

"I appreciate the difficult questions you raised … thanks Bill," offered Mae.

The following Chart (Figure 19) identifies some moral concerns Arthur and the Board faced.

Principled Thinking Model	SCENARIO: Arthur's Moral Dilemma
Duty	Arthur felt he was facing a conflict of duties: closure of the church versus the effect the closure would have on young and old
Rights	Arthur recognized Emma's rights as a human right - a right which people claim they have as human beings
Motive	Arthur made sure that the Board deliberated from a morally good motive, namely, the desire to do what is the right thing to do.
Desert	The Board insisted they did not deserve the kind words from Emma.
Just	The Board concluded that a decision must not only be morally right but it must also be just

Figure 19: Principled Thinking Model applied to Arthur's Moral Dilemma

It is significant that the Board, according to Arthur's recollection, discussed closure of the church with a focus on duties, rights and motive before they arrived at their difficult conclusion to close the church. Arthur seemed to be troubled by this; somehow he felt they may not have considered whether their decision was just considering the special needs of some people like Emma. So, as Chair, he reconvened the Board to review the basis for their decision to close the church. They focused their discussions on the issue: close the church versus provide support to the people in need. This led to a new decision which did not reverse the original decision to close the church. To be just, they decided to replace the church with a community center which could respond to the needs of the local community. The Board's response to Emma's letter of gratitude is interesting. They maintained they did not deserve Emma's kind words.

The following Chart (Figure 20) identifies the moral values principle tests the Board applied as they made their decisions.

MORAL VALUES PRINCIPLE TESTS	SCENARIO: Arthur's Moral Dilemma
New Cases Test	Consider Emma's future
Role Exchange Test	
Subsumption Test	Close the church versus provide support to the people in need after the church is closed
Universal Consequences Test	Who would support people like Emma after the church was closed?

Figure 20: Moral Values Principle Tests applied to Arthur's Moral Dilemma

Arthur was not moved to reflect on the Board's decision based only on sound reasons. He also applied two of the moral values principle tests: subsumption test and universal consequences test. The Board concluded that it was not really facing a conflict of duties. It could do both, close the church and provide support for people in need. This conclusion was driven, in part by considering the universal consequences of closing their church: Who would support people like Emma? In this case, applying the moral values principle tests along with rigorous thinking led to a challenging moral decision: build a community centre to replace the church.

Chapter 17
Cyber Bullying

This chapter addresses a current widespread social problem, cyber bullying, and what to do about it.

Cyber bullying is a serious problem. Many people believe that we need additional laws to control online hate crimes and harassments such as uploading revenge porn or amending a person's Facebook profile. Other online harassment problems include impersonating a victim or posting harmful or private content online in a victim's name. Was the leak of celebrity selfies a crime after the iCloud service was hacked even though people choose to post their own selfies online? There is no consensus on how society should address these problems.

People have defended many excuses for their behavior online but none of them justify their action. Some people feel disconnected from their behaviour towards the victim since cyber bullying occurs anonymously online but that does not make their behavior right. It is wrong whether the harassment occurs once or many times. Whether the harmful websites or fake profile pages are used by a person long after the sites were set up is immaterial; it's still wrong.

Some people ask questions like: "Who is committing a moral or legal offence – the one posting on a website or the one viewing it?" There seems to be no consensus on this question. Some say the one posting it, others say the viewer, and still others say both. Some people maintain interfering with another person's privacy through cyber technology should be treated as a criminal offence. There is no agreement on whether a breach of privacy should be treated more seriously than just considering it as an embarrassment for the victim. However, many agree the behavior should involve significant humiliation such as posting the names of perpetrators online. Computer hacking is already a legal offence. Do we really need more laws or is moral suasion the right action to take[129]?

Conversation – Mae and Bill

"WOW! This story hits close to home," exclaimed Mae. "I certainly have experienced first-hand the pain of cyber bullying."

"What happened?" asked Bill. "Did you post some personal selfies online in Facebook?"

"Yes, so what's your point?" demanded Mae. She didn't like Bill's tone of voice when he asked his question. She continued, "Are you defending hacking? How would you feel if a hacker accessed your selfie and posted it on a porn site?"

"NO, NO!" insisted Bill, "of course not. Cyber bullying has become a much too common form of psychological hurt and worse these days. Apparently almost half of the kids online have been bullied; some people maintain one in four have had it happen to them more than once."

"You are right, cyber bullying is not funny," maintained Mae. "Almost 70% of teens agree that cyber bullying is a serious problem. Four out of five young people think bullying online is easier to get away with than bullying in person."

"Some of the bullying is really serious," added Bill. "especially when it is used to engage in revenge porn, amend a person's Facebook profile or impersonate a victim by posting harmful or private content online in the victim's name."

"It must be stopped. The question is, how can it be stopped?" asked Mae. "Any laws would have to cover so many issues."

"Agreed," said Bill and added, "What if the harassment of a victim occurs only once? Does it have to be repeated to be a legal offence? What if harmful websites or fake profile pages are used by another person long after these sites were set up?"

"Why are you asking these questions which suggest that at some point posting harmful or fake information may not be illegal?" demanded Mae.

Instead of replying to Mae's question, Bill came up with a zinger, "Who is committing a moral or legal offence: the one posting a selfie on the website or the one viewing it?"

"There you go again!" protested Mae. "You are blaming the ones posting selfies on their websites even when they are posted on servers that are private and apparently protected from hackers. You obviously have had no experience with selfies."

"My apologies, I did not mean to criticize you or anyone else posting selfies," assured Bill.

"I think interfering with another person's privacy through cyber technology should be treated as a criminal offence," insisted Mae. "It violates people's rights to express themselves."

"Perpetrators and victims alike need to understand the opportunities and dangers of the Internet," concluded Bill. "At the same time, people posting selfies online need to be treated with respect and fairness."

The tension between Bill and Mae remained even after Bill's reassuring words.

The following Chart (Figure 21) summarizes how Mae and Bill applied the Principled Thinking Model as they struggled with the problem of cyber bullying.

PRINCIPLED THINKING MODEL	SCENARIO: Cyber Bullying	
	Mae	Bill
Duty		It must be stopped.
Rights	It violates people's rights to express themselves.	
Motive	Why are you asking these questions which suggest that at some point posting harmful or fake information may not be illegal?	
Desert		
Just		... people posting selfies online need to be treated with respect and fairness

Figure 21: Principled Thinking Model applied to Cyber Bullying

It is interesting to notice that Mae and Bill focused on different concerns. Mae focused on rights (It violates people's rights to express themselves.) and motive (Why are you asking these questions which suggest that at some point posting harmful or fake information may not be illegal?") and Bill focused on duties (It must be stopped.) and justice (people posting selfies online need to be treated with respect and fairness). Could that be one reason why they seemed to talk past each other? On the other hand, it could have led them to engage in a rich conversation by taking the conversation beyond what each of them brought to it. What might have brought them together to consider the insights each brought to the conversation? Note in the following chart what Mae suggested that could have brought them together – "How would you feel if a hacker posted your selfie on a porn site?). Unfortunately, it didn't.

The following Chart (Figure 22) shows the test Mae used in their discussion of cyber bullying.

MORAL VALUES PRINCIPLE TESTS	SCENARIO: Cyber Bullying
New Cases Test	
Role Exchange Test	How would you feel if a hacker posted your selfie on a porn site?
Subsumption Test	They did not ask this question: What is more important: protecting the freedom of Internet users OR protecting Internet users from harassments?
Universal Consequences Test	

Figure 22: Moral Values Principled Tests applied to Cyber Bullying

Mae seemed to be focused on protecting Internet users from harassments while Bill seemed to be focused on protecting the freedom of access to the Internet. Mae's use of a role exchange question did not bring them together in the conversation. Since Mae personally experienced cyber bullying, they might have considered applying some of the other tests. For example, they might have considered using the Subsumption Test where the discussion would have focused on prioritizing principles or issues. They could have discussed the following apparent conflict between them: What is more important - protecting the freedom of access to the Internet OR protecting Internet users from harassments? It might have led them to the conclusion that both are important. That discussion might have led Mae and Bill to understand and appreciate each other's concerns.

Chapter 18
Civil Society

This chapter shifts to a fundamental national issue: the responsibility of civil society to support services like education and universal health care .

Jeremy Rifkin[130] maintains that society is made up of three major forces – the market place, government and civil society. He points out that we have allowed corporations and the government to address the needs of society. So much so, that whenever we encounter a serious social problem, we immediately appeal to large corporations to make philanthropic donations and to governments for more services or laws to solve social problems.

According to Rifkin, civil societies used to attend to the basic needs of individuals and communities with laws and services in education, health care, recreation and entertainment. They wrote stories about their collective destiny, created codes of conduct, and generated opportunities for establishing bonds of trust which generated social cohesion. This trust and cohesion served as a basis for civil societies to assume responsibility for the welfare of everyone in their communities. The feeling was that nobody should be left behind.

The problem with the market place and government is that they do not build bonds of trust in society, which is essential for creating social cohesion. They each represent a narrow range of values and cultural norms. The market place is driven primarily by the bottom line whereas government's primary role is to maintain law and order. Both are driven essentially by materialistic and utilitarian values, according to Rifkin.

Rifkin maintains that civil societies can build responsible cohesive societies based on a different core value - *by giving of oneself, one's well-being is enhanced.* This could generate the social capital in society for ensuring the well-being of everyone. So, here is the challenge. How can civil society do this?[131.]

Conversation - Mae and Bill

"WOW!" That's a big order for us at the community level - by giving of oneself, one's well-being is enhanced. Come to think of it, just what does that mean? What is Rifkin expecting of our community?" exclaimed Bill. "We have a daughter suffering from a congenital heart disease. Our government has built a local hospital and an international corporation has funded a heart treatment centre costing millions for our local hospital. I appreciate what they have done to meet the needs of people like our daughter. What's left for our community to do?"

"Good question," responded Mae. "I certainly don't have an answer for you. I can think of one more step the government could take. It could hire a number of psychologists to support families who have to cope with serious illness."

"Sure! One more thing that the government can do ... and raise our taxes some more," countered Bill. "What's more, I nor my wife need a psychologist poking around in our lives. That's not going to do anything for us!"

At the same time, Mae was intrigued by Rifkin's suggestion - by giving of oneself, one's well-being is enhanced. What might that mean in practical terms, she wondered. She recalled Rifkin's reference to *building bonds* to *create cohesive societies*. What does that have to do with meeting Bill's needs? So she asked, "What might a community do for or with people when they experience illness in the family?"

"They do all sorts of things," replied Bill. "They drop in to chat, often they bring a snack or even a full meal," recalled Bill. "That's what our neighbours did for us when our daughter was in the hospital."

"Did they do anything for your daughter?" asked Mae. "Did they ..."

Before Mae could complete her sentence, Bill interjected, "Absolutely. They invited her whenever one of her classmates had a birthday party. I remember on one occasion when one of our neighbours asked her to join them for an overnight trip to a national park near-by. Our daughter could not stop talking about the things they did together at the park."

"Oh, one more thing," added Bill. "Whenever we planned a local fun thing to do as a family, our daughter insisted that her friend join us. The two of them had so much fun together. It was a blessing for my wife and myself to see them enjoying each other's company!"

Suddenly it dawned on Mae what Rifkin may have meant when he talked about what a community could do that big hospitals and large corporations could not do. What Bill had just described no doubt enhanced the well-being of everyone involved – Bill's daughter, his family and probably even his neighbours – by supporting each other. That's what generated the *social capital* that bonded them together. What a support in time of need thought Mae. She blurted out, "What you just described about your daughter, your family and your neighbours reminds me of something I read in Nel Nodding's book, *Caring*. She maintained that *caring* is a two-way street where everyone is the-one-caring and the-one-cared-for.

You all cared for each other in whatever ways you could. That's what built the bond which supported your family through the challenges of seeing your daughter suffer through her illness."

"Thanks, Mae," Bill said quietly. "That was really helpful."

The following Chart (Figure 23) summarizes the application of the Principled Thinking Model.

PRINCIPLED THINKING MODEL	SCENARIO: Civil Society	
	Mae	Bill
Duty		That's a big order for us at the community level
Rights		
Motive	by giving of oneself, one's well-being is enhanced	
Desert		
Just		

Figure 23: Principled Thinking Model applied to Civil Society

It is striking that the conversation between Mae and Bill focused primarily on motive - *by giving of oneself, one's well-being is enhanced*. They paid very little attention to duty and none to rights, desert, and justice. Still, the conversation overcame Bill's doubts (What is left for our community to do?) and scepticism about Mae's reference to hiring more psychologists (I nor my wife need a psychologist poking around in our lives.

That's not going to do anything for us). Mae was able to draw on Bill's experience about people caring for each other. This changed Bill's perspective on what communities are in fact able to contribute to people's well-being. In the end Bill said to Mae, "Thanks, Mae. That was really helpful." This scenario suggests that applying the Principled Thinking Model does not require that the entire model has to be applied every time to generate deeper understanding of how to resolve a conflict.

The following Chart (Figure 24) shows the moral values principle tests used by Bill.

MORAL VALUES PRINCIPLE TESTS	SCENARIO: Civil Society
New Cases Test	We have a daughter suffering from a congenital heart disease.
Role Exchange Test	
Subsumption Test	I nor my wife need a psychologist poking around in our lives. That's not going to do anything for us
Universal Consequences Test	by giving of oneself, one's well-being is enhanced

Figure 24: Moral Values Principle Tests applied to Civil Society

Mae and Bill drew on the moral values principle tests in trying to address Bill's question, "What might a community do for or with people when they experience illness in the family?" Bill focused on the immediate situation of their daughter and Mae accepted that reference point. Bill forcefully rejected Mae's suggestion that psychologists be made available to them through government funding. He insisted that they did not need psychologists poking around in their lives. They were grateful for the hospital with a modern heart treatment centre. After Mae walked Bill through sharing his experience in his community, he came to realize the importance of a community. He understood what Rifkin meant when he said - by giving of oneself, one's well-being is enhanced. The well-being of everyone was well served by sharing this core value in the community.

Chapter 19
International Responsibilities

This chapter takes us to an international challenge by raising the question: What responsibilities do nations have in solving each other's challenges of providing social services? In this case, Mae and Bill discuss the responsibility Canadians should or should not assume in providing affordable access to education for children in another country where they do not have access to quality education. In other words, do countries like Canada have an international responsibility to offer essential social services, like education, to children in other countries? Mae says yes and Bill is not so sure.

Let me introduce you to the town of Tenom located in the Interior Division of Sabah, Malaysia on the island of Borneo, home of a majestic rain forest. Tenom is located in the heart of an agricultural area which produces rubber trees, cocoa, palm oil, soy beans, and coffee. This sounds like a prosperous region which produces products in demand around the world. But, as in so many other countries, the local farmers barely make enough money to look after the basic needs of their families. International markets keep the price for these products so low that farmers do not receive fair market value for their produce.

A typical village family income is $250 to $600 Ringgits (Malaysian currency) per month which equals to $90

- $200 Canadian. A two bedroom apartment rents for $150 to $500 Ringgits a month. Hence most village families, which average 4-6 children, build their own homes as best they can. The children have to help in the family vegetable plot or in the rice field after school. Typically they help their parents on Sunday selling vegetables in the town open market square. The local government provides the children with new uniforms and sometimes with shoes as well. The parents have to pay for the school supplies.

Unfortunately, most students do not acquire an adequate command of English in government schools even though English is a compulsory subject in Malaysia and essential to succeed in high school and university. They hear and speak Murut, Chinese, Malay, or Kadazan Dusun at home. To learn to speak and write English well, students need private English tutors which their parents cannot afford.

High school and university students need a good command of oral and written English to be able to leave the marginal farms and get jobs in the cities. The local government sponsors some high school students each year by paying for their school supplies and room and board. Students who speak and write English get to the top of the sponsorship list. The rest of the students are unable to attend high school or university[132].

In today's global communication networks people in affluent countries like Canada know about situations in third world countries like Malaysia. Does it follow that affluent countries like Canada should assume an active role in ensuring that children in developing countries have access to the education they need? Bill is not so sure that Canadian taxpayers should subsidize the education of children in other countries to get out of the poverty of their parents.

Conversation – Mae and Bill

"As a Canadian who has access to a high quality education system, what comes to mind when you read this report about the educational future of students in Malaysia?" asked Mae.

"Are you asking me what, I think, Canadians ought to do about the lack of adequate educational opportunities in Tenom? Are you suggesting that Canada has a duty to respond given its quality education? Of course Canada has a duty to provide educational opportunities for Canadians. But, why is Canada obligated to extend this service to children in Tenom?" asked Bill.

"Why not," replied Mae.

"It seems that Canada would then be obligated to provide educational opportunities for all communities around the world where children are in need of quality education but don't have access to it. That goal would be impossible to achieve!" argued Bill.

"Maybe Canada has a responsibility to support educational opportunities for some needy children because it has an excellent education system," replied Mae.

"Are you suggesting that if an act is morally right, it is a person's duty to do it? I don't think that follows. Just because it is morally right to offer educational services to children in Malaysia, it does not necessarily follow that Canada has a duty to do it," argued Bill.

"But, if it were Canada's duty to provide affordable educational opportunities, it would be wrong not to do it," replied Mae.

"So, if Canada has a duty to support educational opportunities abroad, would Tenom have a right to demand support from Canada?" asked Bill.

"I see where you are going," acknowledged Mae. "If Tenom has that right based on Canada's duty, then every community in need of educational opportunities might have that right. I recognize that that would not be realistic. At the same time, Canada might decide to go beyond the call of duty and support one community, say Tenom," suggested Mae.

"But what would Canada's motive be for doing that?" asked Bill. "Would Canada be motivated by the desire to do what's right or by a good motive such as compassion for the young people living in Tenom who are unable to get an education?"

"What do you think?" asked Mae. No response from Bill. "There is no doubt in my mind that Canada would be motivated by a sense of fairness in providing equal educational opportunities to children and young people in Tenom to the extent that Canada can afford it. They need a good education just like the students in Canada," maintained Mae.

"But once again, Canada needs to consider the universal consequences of being fair to one country," maintained Bill. "I ask again, would Canada be obligated to support quality education in all countries where children do not have access to quality education?"

"Obviously, there is no simple answer to that challenge. Canada could consider offering educational support in one community in Malaysia. In fact, the educational program offered in Malaysia through Sponsor a Village is a good Canadian example. It has received over three million hits from nearly 400,000 users around the word," observed Mae.

Bill and Mae were unable to resolve this dilemma even though they agreed that they had clarified the issue of nations assuming some international responsibility for providing an essential service such as education to communities in need in other countries.

The Chart (Figure 25) below identifies the categories of the Principled Thinking Model used by Mae and Bill.

PRINCIPLED THINKING MODEL	SCENARIO: International Responsibilities	
	Mae	Bill
Duty	- Maybe Canada has a responsibility by virtue of its particular position as a country with an excellent education system - If it were Canada's duty, it would be wrong not to do it. - Canada might decide to go beyond the call of duty.	- Are you suggesting that Canada has a duty to support educational opportunities abroad? - What ought Canadians do about the lack of adequate educational opportunities in Tenom? - Why is Canada obligated to extend this service to Tenom? - It seems that Canada would then be obligated to provide educational opportunities for all communities around the world
Rights	If Tenom has that right based on Canada's duty, then every community might have that right	- if Canada has a duty to support educational opportunities abroad, would Tenom have a right?
Motive	What would Canada's motive be for doing that?	Would Canada be motivated by the desire to do right or be motivated by a good motive such as compassion?
Desert		
Just	Canada would be motivated by a sense of fairness.	

Figure 25: Principled Thinking Model applied to International Responsibilities

Mae and Bill were involved in a rich exchange involving the categories of the Principled Thinking Model except *desert*. Although they did not arrive at a mutually agreed upon solution for the dilemma they faced, they offered a thorough analysis of the duties and rights in the case. They even explored the relationship between *duty* and *rights* through Bill's question, "If Canada has a duty to support educational opportunities abroad, would Tenom have a right?"

The following Chart (Figure 26) shows which moral values principle test was applied.

MORAL VALUES PRINCIPLE TESTS	SCENARIO: International Responsibilities
New Cases Test	
Role Exchange Test	
Subsumption Test	
Universal Consequences Test	- Canada needs to consider the universal consequences of being fair to one country - It seems to follow that Canada would then be obligated to provide educational opportunities for all communities in need around the world

Figure 26: Moral Values Principle Tests applied to
International Responsibilities

Mae and Bill used one moral values principle test in their discussion by considering the universal consequences of Canada being obligated to provide educational services for students in need in other countries. If Canada needs to consider the universal consequences of being fair to one country, it seems to follow that Canada would then be obligated to provide educational opportunities for all communities in need around the world. That clearly did not seem plausible.

Mae was troubled by their discussion; she could not understand Bill's reluctance to consider Canada's responsibilities in offering educational support to children in third world countries. So she followed up on what she could do on her own. She supported an online education program, Sponsor a Village, which offers lessons, assignments, and answer keys on English grammar and writing (beginner – Collage entrance). Imagine how much more Mae could accomplish if she had been able to convince Bill of the merits of providing educational support for needy children in other countries. He might have joined her in her project.

Chapter 20
The Enemy Is Neglect of Mental Illness

This Chapter addresses a situation that is complicated by the fact that it involves a person suffering from mental illness.

> On Dec. 15, 2011, Michael Zehaf-Bibeau walked into a Burnaby RCMP detachment office and asked to be arrested for a robbery he claimed to have committed 10 years ago. He was briefly detained under B.C.'s Mental Health Act but later released. Hours later he attempted to rob a local McDonalds restaurant with a sharpened stick —an act so bizarre the fast food employee thought he was joking.

> Michael apparently had a long history of addiction and mental illness. On one occasion, he asked a B.C. judge to send him to jail so that he could deal with his addiction to crack cocaine. The judge indulged him with a brief jail term over the Christmas holidays.

> A court psychiatrist determined that "although he seems to be making an unusual choice, this was an insufficient basis for a diagnosis of mental disorder. In order to be admitted to a treatment facility under the Canadian Mental Health Association, BC Division, Michael would have to suffer from a condition that "seriously impairs the person's ability to react appropriately to the person's environment, or to associate with others[133]."

Michael's case reflects a yawning crack in the Canadian mental health care system. People like Michael fall between the specific criteria as set by the Canadian Mental Health Association and the services available by police who are not trained to respond to people suffering from mental illness.

Conversation - Mae and Bill

"So what are the yawning cracks in the Canadian health care system?" asked Bill.

"Where do I begin?" thought Mae out loud. "Put yourself in Michael's shoes and you will soon find out," insisted Mae.

"What's that supposed to mean?" said Bill with a smirk on his face.

"Well, imagine asking for permission to spend some time in a jail cell to deal with your cocaine addiction! Do you know of anyone who has asked for that?" demanded Mae.

"No," replied Bill. "Nor are any of my friends drug addicts."

"Imagine suffering from mental illness and being so desperate that the only way out is to ask to be admitted to a jail," challenged Mae.

"Why didn't he go to a hospital Emergency to ask for help?" asked Bill.

"You must be kidding me," Mae shot back. "For all we know, he tried that in the past and was never admitted."

"Why not?" asked Bill.

"I have no idea," said Mae. "In any case, apparently the staff at the jail did not refer him to Emergency. They simply granted him a brief stay in a jail cell. Come to think of it, I recall a friend of mine who was suffering from drug addiction. On one occasion when he was at a low point in his addicted life, he went to a hospital Emergency and pleaded for help.

What did they do for him? They gave him a hand full of pills and sent him home! That's the kind of help he got from Emergency."

"Maybe it's that difficult to determine whether a person is suffering from mental illness or just having a bad day," responded Bill.

"Hospital should have the same obligation to meet the medical needs of people suffering from mental illness as someone who arrives in Emergency with a broken leg. People suffering from mental illness surely have the same rights as any other person. The staff at the jail probably would be the first to insist that people suffering from mental illness deserve better. But, that's the system ... it is so unfair," observed Mae.

Bill's limited appreciation for people suffering from mental illness was deeply troubling to Mae.

Note the categories used by Mae to discuss the gap in the services provided for people suffering from mental illness (Figure 27).

PRINCIPLED THINKING MODEL	SCENARIO: The Enemy Is Neglect of Mental Illness	
	Mae	Bill
Duty	Hospital should have the same obligation to meet the medical needs of people suffering from mental illness as someone who arrives in Emergency with a broken leg.	
Rights	People suffering from mental illness surely have the same rights as any other person.	

Motive		
Desert	The staff at the jail probably would be the first to insist that people suffering from mental illness deserve better	
Justice	But, that's the system ... it is so unfair	

Figure 27: Principled Thinking Model applied to
The Enemy Is Neglect of Mental Illness

Mae was focused on duties, rights, desert and justice in her effort to help Bill understand the cracks in the mental health services for people suffering from mental illness. She was clearly frustrated by Bill's lack of appreciation and empathy for a group of people who are not receiving necessary health care.

Does Bill reflect a common perception of people suffering from mental illness? Is that one reason why they experience a 70-90% unemployment rate? Do first responders, like police officers and hospital admission staff as well as employers, need training in recognizing the symptoms of mental illness? Many questions were left unanswered.

The following Chart (Figure 28) shows the moral values principle tests used by Mae.

MORAL VALUES PRINCIPLE TESTS	SCENARIO: The Enemy Is Neglect of Mental Illness
New Cases Test	- I recall a friend of mine who was suffering from drug addiction. On one occasion when he was at a low point in his addicted life, he went to a hospital Emergency and pleaded for help
Role Exchange Test	- Put yourself in Michael's shoes and you will soon find out. - Imagine asking for permission to spend some time in a jail cell to deal with you cocaine addiction.
Subsumption Test	
Universal Consequences Test	

Figure 28: Moral Values Principle Tests applied to
The Enemy Is Neglect of Mental Illness

Mae used moral values principle tests to help Bill understand the challenges facing people suffering from mental illness. Mae used a new case (I recall a friend) and role exchange (put yourself in Michael's shoes) to help Bill feel Michael's pain and hopefully empathize with him. But, to no avail. Obviously, it will take more than one conversation to convince Bill of the dilemma people suffering from mental illness face, including the pain of massive unemployment.

Chapter 21
Reconciliation

The Canadian Government assumed the responsibility not only for providing an education for First Nations children, but also to assimilate them into the white Anglo-Saxon culture. To accomplish both goals, the government introduced residential schools where First Nations children had to live in residence away from their communities and families with the goal of expediting the assimilation process. Attending these schools, which were run federally under the Department of Indian Affairs, was compulsory; attendance was enforced by government agents.

CBC CANADA[134] described the children's experience as follow: "When students returned to the reserve, they often found they didn't belong. They didn't have the skills to help their parents, and became ashamed of their native heritage. The skills taught at the schools were generally substandard. Many children found it hard to function in an urban setting. Many were subjected to years of abuse. Consequently, assimilation meant devastation for the First Nations children."

A Truth and Reconciliation Commission was established by the Canadian government with a mandate to "document the extent and impact of residential school experiences; to provide a safe setting for former students to share their stories; and to produce a report to the federal government on the legacy of the residential school system[135]."

This is the experience of First Nations children residential schools.

Verna Flanders was just six years old when she was sent to a residential school. Up to that point, the young girl, whose mother had died in childbirth, had been cared for by her aunt and uncle.

"... I came into the wrong hands when I was six," Flanders told the Truth and Reconciliation Commission. She described the sense of sheer isolation and loneliness she felt as a boarding student at St. Michael's Indian Residential School in Alert Bay.

For 10 years, she missed out on typical childhood experiences, like knowing what it is like to celebrate a birthday, or going home to see her family for Christmas. She grew up without family, spending a decade of her life, as she remembers it, "behind brick walls".

"I felt so alone," she said, through tears. "I had no one." And, when she left the school at 16, there was no one there to meet her.

Andre Hannon, in Commission Seeks Truth, reports that "over the century that the residential schools operated, thousands of children from about five or six to about 16 were taken away from their families and subjected to horrific psychological, physical and sexual abuse, leaving a legacy of dysfunction that has been passed down to the second and third generations ... Nearly 150,000 children went through 90 schools across the country; up to 4,000 children died in these schools[136]."

Conversation – Mae and Bill

"Verna's personal story is too much for me; I cannot imagine what it must have been like to grow up without loving parents and as she remembers it behind brick walls," said Mae almost in tears and barely audible. "I simply cannot express my sorrow and empathy for Verna in the way we have been discussing other problems. I don't know what to say."

Bill was touched by Mae's sincere emotions; he was speechless. After a few awkward moments of silence, he found himself agreeing with Mae, "Somehow, expressing our emotions needs to be part of our conversation."

"I feel a deep sense of empathy" responded Mae, "not only for Verna but for the tens of thousands who suffered like her or worse. Without both, thinking about her experience and feeling her pain, I am unable to express myself adequately."

"Maybe we should find out what the Truth and Reconciliation Commission recommended," suggested Bill.

"The name of the Commission suggests a way forward: truth and reconciliation," observed Mae. "For openers," said Mae, "it would be important for me to determine the obligations of the people responsible for what happened to the children ... to get to the truth."

"How could children like Verna ever be compensated for the wrong done to them ... and restore their rights?" asked Bill.

"They deserve more than just compensation for the loss of their rights," insisted Mae.

"What would that be besides sharing a sense of dignity and respect for one another?" queried Bill.

"It probably includes a reciprocal relationship between the one-caring (the people operating the schools) and the one-cared-for (First Nations people). Both parties need to support each other. That might be a promising path towards reconciliation," offered Mae.

"I guess that could lead to a better life for both parties well beyond merely co-existing," observed Bill.

"Maybe that's why they did not call the Commission, The Fairness Commission. They wanted much more than being fair to First Nations people," chimed Mae. "The Commission wanted the dominant white population become aware of the pain they had inflicted on First Nations children with the hope that this awareness would lead to reconciliation.

"Come to think of it," concluded Bill, "maybe we should have considered empathy in all our conversations on the various issues we discussed."

"I couldn't agree with you more. Absolutely," Mae replied.

Mae and Bill used the Principled Thinking Model to address reconciliation (Figure 29).

PRINCIPLED THINKING MODEL	SCENARIO: Reconciliation	
	Mae	Bill
Duty	- Determine the obligations of the people responsible for what happened to the children.	
Rights		- Restore their (First Nations people) rights.
Motive		
Desert	They (First Nations people) deserve more than just compensation	

Just	The Commission wanted much more than being fair to First Nations.	

Figure 29: Principled Thinking Model applied to Reconciliation

Imagine wanting more than what a Fairness Commission would have to offer! With this observation, Mae was leading towards the need to include a sense of empathy in addressing the pain suffered by First Nations children. However, I think Mae captured the essence of reconciliation in her statement: [*Engage*] *in a reciprocal relationship between the one-caring and the one-cared-for*. Both parties need to support each other. In other words, both parties, the dominant white population and the First Nations people, need to recognize that they both need to care for and support each other. The dominant white population needs to work together with First Nations people to create a wholesome and healthy environment that takes into account the aspirations and cultures of both people. That might be a promising path towards reconciliation. I think that is what Mae had in mind.

The following Chart (Figure 30) identifies the moral values principle tests that Mae and Bill applied.

MORAL VALUES PRINCIPLE TESTS	SCENARIO: Reconciliation
New Cases Test	
Role Exchange Test	I cannot imagine what it must have been like to grow up without loving parents.
Subsumption Test	

Universal Consequences Test	That could lead to a quality of life for both parties.

Figure 30: Moral Values Principle Tests applied to Reconciliation

The application of moral values principle tests helped Mae and Bill grasp the emotional tension involved in trying to understand Verna's experience growing up in a residential school. It had been so different from their childhood experience; both had grown up in supportive families and communities. The First Nations children, on the other hand, had been ripped from their families and culture to live in a strange culture under duress. Grasping the emotional stress of their experience is the first step to recognizing that both need to care for and support each other. That was the initial goal of the Truth and Reconciliation Commission.

Part IV
What if ...

Back to my journey I described in the Introduction. The scenarios and reports convince me of the importance of applying both, the Principled Thinking Model and the Moral Values Principle Tests in an effort to resolve moral dilemmas in pursuit of justice. Some scenarios (The Irate Parent) demonstrate the problem of not applying them effectively. Some (The Considerate parent) reflect the *slow thinking* recommended by Daniel Kahneman by engaging in a discussion about moral dilemmas before facing moments of decisions. Some (Access to the Internet) reflect the failure to ask many related questions which might have resulted in a more comprehensive discussion of a moral dilemma. The resolution of a moral dilemma by applying both, the model and the tests, was demonstrated in Arthur's Moral Dilemma. Mae and Bill's profound discussion of the Truth and Reconciliation Commission Report reflected a deep insight into what is entailed in *reconciliation*. I could go on but these examples make the point – I needed to go beyond the Principled Thinking Model where I focused on the *cognitive* demands of resolving moral dilemmas in pursuit of justice and acknowledge the critical foundation *empathy* provides for resolving moral dilemmas in pursuit of justice.

At the same time, we must never forget the critical importance of *thinking* through moral dilemmas in pursuit of justice. That's why I close with the question: "What if we don't engage in slow or deep thinking? Could we end up in 2084 like this?"

It's 2084 ... the post Kurzweil era of Singularity is NOW. Bob, who owns a thriving company located in Kingston, Ontario, has just confirmed via ThoughtNet that his 3D printers, the first ThoughtProgramme printers, are ready for shipping to a major client, Zen Virtual, in Uzbekistan. This shipment is part of a major international transaction where Bob's company will receive in exchange a shipment of nanobots for distribution in North America.

Bob got interested in this transaction partly for the business opportunity it offered but also because nanobots could save him personally from an agonising death from cancer. Nanobots not only monitor the body for any rogue cancer cells, but instantly destroy them and replace them with healthy identical cells using the DNA of the rogue cells.

Bob has just detected a problem via ThoughtNet. The Vice President of Zen Virtual, Dr. Scruples, is devising a scheme whereby his company plans to direct part of Bob's nanobot order to a virtual warehouse in Shanghai. Apparently, Dr. Scruples has no scruples ... he is quite prepared to shortchange Bob's company of half the order of nanobots but bill him for the full order. Within minutes of this discovery, Bob confronted Dr. Scruples about the ThoughtMessage which Bob discovered on ThoughtNet.

Dr. Scruples replied with utter surprise at Bob's consternation. Why would he be upset with Zen Virtual for trying to execute the best transaction possible? Now Bob was really worried. Upon further investigation, he discovered to his astonishment that Dr. Scruples has no conscience or sense of right and wrong. His digital brain had been programmed by virtual ThoughtProgrammers who had never been introduced to MoralThought thinking.

Bob was crushed. He knew he could not do business with Dr. Scruples who had no scruples. He cancelled the order and continued to suffer the ravages of cancer[137].

I created this scenario based on the exponential growth of digital computing power as presented by Ray Kurzweil, one of the world's leading inventors, thinkers, and futurist. He maintains that "The combination of human-level intelligence with a computer's inherent superiority in speed, accuracy, and memory-sharing ability will be formidable[138]." This may be achieved after all functions of the human brain have been discovered so that a digital brain can be created through reverse engineering. Kurzweil claims that could be achieved in the twenty first century which would set the stage for the scenario described above.

My concern is about the apparent absence of any serious research on enabling the digital brain to exercise moral reasoning in the context of a sense of empathy which I maintain is essential for resolving moral dilemmas in pursuit of justice. As I mention in the Introduction, digital engineers can develop software for self-driving cars which can make cost-benefit decisions; but, they are not yet able to make moral decisions based on careful reflections and a sense of empathy. Both are necessary for addressing the human need for fair and caring resolutions of moral dilemmas.

Whether Ray Kurzweil is right about his best estimate that neuroscientists will have discovered all the functions of the brain by 2030 thus enabling the development of a digital brains to engage in ThoughtNets; or Stephen Hawkings[139], theoretical physicist and cosmologist, is right when he claims that "if humans develop a computer with full artificial intelligence, it could spell the end of the human race"; or Darren Abramson[140], Philosopher and Cognitive Scientist, is right when he maintains "no one should lose sleep over this", we need to remind ourselves of the categories and concepts needed to answer questions about right and wrong in order to resolve moral dilemmas in pursuit of justice. The 2084 scenario offers one example of the kind of world we can envision in the absence of a society based on justice and caring.

So, let's remember:

Caring emotions are informed by thought;

Moral thought is powered by caring emotions.

Reference

1. "11 Facts about Cyber Bullying", Dosomething.org, https://www.dosomething.org/us/facts/11-facts-about-cyber -bullying.

2. A history of residential schools in Canada" CBC NEWS (Mar 21, 2016). http://www.cbc.ca/news/canada/a-history-of-residential-schools-in-canada-1.702280

3. Attorney General of Ontario, *Ontario Human Rights Commission*. Toronto: Ontario, 1962.

4. Anderson, Mitchell, "The Enemy Is Neglect of Mental Illness." *The Tyee*, October 25, 2014. https://www.google.ca/search?q=1.+Anderson%2C+Mitchell%2C+ %E2%80%9CThe+Enemy+Is+Neglect+of+Mental+Illness.%E2%8 0%9D&rlz=1C1GGGE_enCA405CA406&oq=1.+Anderson%2C+M itchell%2C+%E2%80%9CThe+Enemy+Is+Neglect+of+Mental+Ill ness.%E2%80%9D&aqs=chrome..69i57.1095j0j1&sourceid=chrom e&ie=UTF-8#q=Anderson%2C+Mitchell%2C+%E2%80%9CThe+E nemy+Is+Neglect+of+Mental+Illness.%E2%80%9D

5. Armstrong, Alison, and Charles Casement, *the child and the Machine*. Toronto: Key Porter Books, 1998.

6. Baier, Kurt, *The Moral Point of* View. New York: Random House, 1965.

7. *Beauregard, Mario, brain wars. Toronto: Harper Collins, 2012.*

8. Bogage, Jacob, "Tesla driver using autopilot killed in crash," *The Washington Post*, June 20, 2016.

9. Bor, Daniel, *Ravenous Brain*. New York: Basic Books, 2012.

10. Brockman, John, *Thinking*. New York: Harper-Collins, 2013.

11. Brooks, David, "If It Feels Right ...", *The New York Times,*" September 12, 2011.

12. Brooks, David, *Road to Character*. New York: Random House, 2015.

13. Cohen, Richard, "Miley Cyrus, Steubenville and teen culture run amok," *Washington Post*, September 2, 2013. https://www.washingtonpost.com/opinions/richard-cohen-miley-cyrus-steubenville-and-culture-run-amok/2013/09/02/1cecafa6-11af-11e3-bdf6-e4fc677d94a1_story.html.

14. Damagio, Antonio, *Self Comes to Mind*. New York: Vintage, 2012.

15. Doidge, Norman, *The Brain that Changes Itself*. New York: Penguin Books, 2007.

16. Festinger, Leon, A *Theory of Cognitive Dissonance*. Stanford: Stanford University Press, 1957.

17. Freeze, D. Richard, "Writing for Meaning." Unpublished, University of Manitoba, 1990.

18. _____, "Writing for Meaning in an Integrated Learning Environment Project." Unpublished, University of Manitoba, 1991.

19. _____, "Writing for Meaning in an Integrated Learning Environment Project: Teachers' and Students' Perceptions." Unpublished, University of Manitoba, 1991.

20. _____, "Integrating Thinking and Writing on the Electronic Page, Writing for Meaning in an Integrated Learning Environment Project." Unpublished, University of Manitoba, 1992.

21. —————————, "Networking for Thinking and Writing: An Evaluation for Students' Reflective Writing in the Networking for Learning Project." Unpublished, University of Manitoba, 1994.

22. —————————, "Writing for Meaning in an Integrated Learning Environment Project." Unpublished, University of Manitoba, 1999.

23. Glassen, Peter, "Are there unresolvable moral disputes?" *Dialogue*, 1:1 (1962): 36 – 50.

24. —————————, "Charientic Judgements." *Philosophy* 33: 125 (1958): 138 – 46.

25. —————————, "The Classes of Moral Terms." *Methodos* KL 43 (1959): 223 – 44.

26. —————————. 1959. "The Cognitivity of Moral Judgements." *Mind*, LXVIII: 269 (1959) 57 – 72.

27. Gilligan, Carol, *In a Different Voice*. Cambridge: Harvard University Press, 1982.

28. Haidt, Jonathan, *The Righteous Mind*. New York: Vintage Books, 2012.

29. Harari, Yuval, Noah, *Homo Deus: A Brief History of Tomorrow*. Toronto: Signal: McClelland & Stewart, 2016.

30. Harari, Yuval Noah, *Sapiens: A Brief History of Mankind*. Toronto: Signal, McClelland & Stewart, 2012

31. Hood, Bruce, *The Self Illusion: How the Social Brain Creates Identity*. Toronto: Harper-Collins, 2013.

32. Hume, David, *Treatise of Human Nature*. London: Dover Publication, 1738.

33. Justin Pritchard. "Google Driverless Car Sideswipes Bus, Gets Caught On Video." THE CANADIAN PRESS, March 10, 2016. http://www.huffingtonpost.ca/2016/03/10/google-driverless-car-bus-accident-video_n_9426134.htmll.

34. *Kahneman, Daniel, Thinking, Fast and Slow. Toronto: Anchor Canada, 2013.*

35. Kohlberg, Lawrence, "Claim to moral adequacy of a highest stage of moral judgment." *Journal of Philosophy*, Vol. 70, January-December (1973) 636 – 637

36. Kohlberg, Lawrence and Rochelle Mayer. "Development as the Aim of Education," *Harvard Educational Review*, Vol. 42, No. 4 (1972). 449-496

37. Kohlberg, Lawrence, "Stages of Moral Development as a basis for moral education." In *Moral Education: Interdisciplinary Approached*, edited by C. H. Beck, B. S. Crittenden, E. V. Sullivan, 23-92. Toronto: University of Toronto Press, 1971.

38. Kurzweil, Ray, *Singularity is Near*. London: Penguin Books, 2005.

39. _____, *How to Create a Mind*. London: Penguin Books, 2012.

40. Keyes, Daniel, *Flowers for Algernon*. New York: Harcourt, 1959.

41. Martin, Robert, *The Opposable Mind*. Boston: Harvard Business Press, 2009.

42. Modgil, Sohan, and Celia Modgil, *Lawrence Kohlberg Consensus and Controversy*. Philadelphia: The Falmer Press, 1986.

43. Nodding, Nel, *Caring*. Berkeley: University of California Press, 1084.

44. Piaget, Jean, "Intellectual Evolution from Adolescence to Adulthood." *Human Development* 15. Basil: Switzerland, 1972.

45. _____, *The Moral Judgment of the Child*. London: Rutledge and Kegan Paul, 1968.

46. Pinker, Steven, *The Better Angels of our Nature*. New York: Penguin Books, 2011.

47. Rawls, John, *Theory of Justice*. Cambridge: Harvard University Press, 1973.

48. Ridley, Matt, *The Rational Optimist*. New York: Harper-Collins, 2010.

49. Rifkin, Jeremy, *The Empathic Civilization*. New York: Jeremy P. Tarcher/Penguin, 2009.

50. Schmidt, Eric and Jared Cohen, *The New Digital Age*. New York: Alfred A. Knopf, 2013.

51. Shermer, Michael, *The Believing Brain*. New York: Henry Holt and Company, 2011.

52. _____, *The Moral Arc*. New York: Henry Holt and Company, 2015.

53. "Stephen Hawking's warning on artificial intelligence long way off." Directed by Alex Mason. CBC News, December 4, 2014.

54. "Study Guide Questions for Reconciling All Things." http://www.ivpress.com/title/disc/3451.pdf

55. Taleb, Nassim Nicholas, *The Black Swan*. New York: Random House Trade Paperback Edition, 2010.

56. Thagard, Paul, *The Brain and the Meaning of Life*. New Jersey: Princeton University Press, 2010.

57. "The Public Schools Act.". C.C.S.M. c. P250, Manitoba, 2015.

58. "The Universal Declaration of Human Rights," UN General Assembly, 1948.

59. Thompson, Clive, *Smarter Than You Think*. New York: The Penguin Press, 2013.

60. Toews, Otto, B, *Discretion and Justice in Educational Administration: Towards a Normative Conceptual Framework*. PhD diss., University of Manitoba, 1981.

61. _____, "Japanese Canadian Story" (CD). Unpublished. Winnipeg: KnowledgeBuilder Software Inc., 1994.

62. _____, *Providence Collage: Online Writing Tutors*. Unpublished. Winnipeg: KnowledgeBuilder Software Inc., 2002.

63. _____, "Sponsor a Village." Vancouver: La Bohème Consulting. Last modified 2016. www.sponsoravillage.ca.

64. _____, *Youth, Law and Morality: A Program in Moral and Legal Education*. Masters thesis, Winnipeg: University of Manitoba, 1975.

65. _____, and Robert Cross, *Multi-media*-KnowledgeBuilder. Software. Winnipeg: KnowledgeBuilder Software Inc., 1994.

66. _____, and _____, *Writers'* KnowledgeBuilder. Software. Winnipeg: KnowledgeBuilder. 1989.

67. _____, McCreath, Joan, *English 2020: College Writing and Grammar*. Unpublished. Winnipeg: KnowledgeBuilder Software Inc., 2008.

68. _____, _____, *English 2020: High School Writing and Grammar*. Unpublished. Winnipeg: KnowledgeBuilder Software Inc., 2008.

69. _____, _____, *Think More ... Write More*. Unpublished. Winnipeg: KnowledgeBuilder Software Inc., 1997.

70. _____, _____, *Room to Read and Write*. Unpublished. Winnipeg: KnowledgeBuilder Software Inc., 2006.

71. "Truth and Reconciliation". Winnipeg: Truth and Reconciliation Commission of Canada, 2015.

72. Yolanda Cole, "Residential school survivors share their stories at Truth and Reconciliation event in Vancouver", Straight (September 21, 2013). http://www.straight.com/news/428331/residential-school-survivors-share-their-stories-truth-and-reconciliation-event-vancouver.

73. Zakaluk, Beverly, "Networking for Learning." Unpublished. University of Manitoba, 1994.
_____. "Sun Valley School Reading and Writing Assessment Report." Unpublished. Winnipeg: University of Manitoba, 1995.

74. _____, The EXCEL Project. Unpublished. University of Manitoba, 1997.

75. _____ and Donna M. Heyday, "The EXCEL Project: Effectiveness of a Wireless laptop computer-based intervention on the biography writing of grade five students." Unpublished. Winnipeg: University of Manitoba, 1998.

Acknowledgements

Over the years, many colleagues have prompted me to pursue challenging issues in my career and in my studies. Dr. Robert Cross encouraged me not only to address difficult educational issues like literacy but also to pursue the application of digital technology for teaching and learning.

Professor Terrence Morrison challenged me through hours of discussions to think critically and by inviting me to participate in conversation with professors across Canada and the US.

Professor Anthony Riffel challenged and coached me through my doctoral program and beyond. He became a trusted friend.

The Principled Thinking Model, which serves as the foundation of this book, is based on the challenging seminars on moral philosophy conducted by Professor Glassen.

Thank you to Apple Canada for a substantial grant to support the development and piloting of a digital thinking and writing environment with the support of Dr. Milt Petrik and Mr. Frank Lechner.

Ten years of pilot studies under the watchful and professional eyes of Dr. Richard Freeze and Dr. Beverly Zakaluk determined the effectiveness of 'to think as you write and write as you think'.

Thank you to many teachers for your diligent involvement in the pilot studies. Your feedback was invaluable.

Years of graduate studies were made possible through two sabbatical leaves granted by my employer, River East School Division, Winnipeg, Manitoba. Thank you.

Thank you, Brendan Gemmell, graduate student at Dalhousie University, for your valuable feedback.

Thank you, Hayley Evans, freelance writer and editor, for challenging me to explore moral issues in the context of problems people face in the real world every day.

Thank you, Astra Crompton, project management and creative coach, for successfully coaching me through the process of publishing a book from the editing assessment to the final product.

I deeply appreciate the countless hours of critical discussions and editing generously offered by my wife, Joan McCreath, Thank you for your steady support, wisdom, and endless patience.

In short, this book was made possible through the collaboration of many contributors. I am proud to have been part of this network. At the same time, I assume full responsibility for any errors and omissions in this book.

I am saddened at the unexpected loss of my son, Konrad, avid reader and debater, who did not live to read this book. His footprint throughout the book is evident to me. Fortunately, my daughter, Eleanor, provides comfort, perceptive inspiration, and love.

End Notes

Preface

[1] David Brooks, "If It Feels Right ... ." *The New York Times*," September 12, 2011.

[2] Paul Thagard, *The Brain and the Meaning of Life* (New Jersey: Princeton University Press, 2010), 254. For a review of the scope and limitation of the use of thought experiments, go to James Robert Brown and Yiftach Fehige, "Thought Experiment", Stanford Encyclopedia of Philosophy, (2014) at https://plato.stanford.edu/entries/thought-experiment/. They raise this challenging question about thought experiments: "The primary philosophical challenge of thought experiments is simple: How can we learn about reality (if we can at all), just by thinking?" They maintain that "most philosophers "recognize them as an occasionally potent tool for increasing our understanding of nature."

[3] Nassim Nicholas Taleb, *The Black Swan*. (New York: Random House Trade Paperback Edition 2010) and John Rawls, *Theory of Justice* (Cambridge: Harvard University Press, 1973).

[4] Baier, Kurt, *The Moral Point of* View (New York: Random House, 1965).

Introduction

[5] "Sponsor a Village" is posted at www.sponsoravillage.ca.

[6] Otto, B. Toews, *Youth, Law and Morality: A Program in Moral and Legal Education*. Masters thesis, University of Manitoba, 1975).

[7] Lawrence Kohlberg and Rochelle Mayer, "Development as the Aim of Education," *Harvard Educational Review*, Vol. 42, No. 4 (1972): 449-496.

[8] Otto, B. Toews and Robert Cross, *Writing for Meaning*. (Unpublished, River East School Division, 1989). Third party researchers prepared the

following unpublished reports on the students' performance when they used writing and thinking strategies as they wrote essays and reports – Richard D. Freeze, "Writing for Meaning, (Unpublished, University of Manitoba, 1990); "Writing for Meaning in an Integrated Learning Environment Project" (Unpublished, University of Manitoba, 1991); "Writing for Meaning in an Integrated Learning Environment Project: Teachers' and Students' Perceptions," (Unpublished, University of Manitoba, 1991); "Thinking and Writing on the Electronic Page, Writing for Meaning in an Integrated Learning Environment Project," (Unpublished, University of Manitoba, 1992); "Networking for Thinking and Writing An Evaluation for Students' Reflective Writing in the Networking for Learning Project," (Unpublished, University of Manitoba, 1994); "Writing for Meaning in an Integrated Learning Environment Project," (Unpublished, University of Manitoba, 1999); and Beverly Zakaluk, "Networking for Learning," (Unpublished, University of Manitoba, 1994); "Sun Valley School Reading and Writing Assessment Report" (Unpublished, University of Manitoba 1995); "The EXCEL Project," (Unpublished, University of Manitoba, 1997), and Donna M. Heyday, "The EXCEL Project: Effectiveness of a Wireless laptop computer-based intervention on the biography writing of grade five students," Unpublished, (Unpublished, University of Manitoba, 1998).

[9] Otto B. Toews and Robert Cross, *Writers' KnowledgeBuilder*. Software (Winnipeg,: KnowledgeBuilder Software Inc. 1989). Dr. Cross wrote a detailed manual on how to use this platform to write stories, essays and reports.

[10]_____, and _____, *Multi-media KnowlegeBuilder*. Software (Winnipeg: KnowledgeBuilder, 1994). Dr. Toews wrote a manual for this software.

[11]Otto B. Toews, "Japanese Canadian Story" (CD). Unpublished, KnowledgeBuilder Software Inc., 1994.

[12] Alison Armstrong and Charles Casement, *the child and the Machine* (Toronto: Key Porter Books, 1998).

[13] Peter Glassen, "Are there unresolvable moral disputes?" *Dialogue,* 1:1 (1962): 36 – 50; "Charientic Judgements." *Philosophy* 33: 125 (1958): 138 – 46; "The Classes of Moral Terms." *Methodos* KL 43 (1959): 223 – 44,

and "The Cognitivity of Moral Judgements." *Mind*, LXVIII: 269 (1959): 57 – 72.

[14] Lawrence Kohlberg and Rochelle Mayer, "Development as the Aim of Education". *Harvard Educational Review*, Volume 42, Number 4. (1972): 154.

[15] Brooks, "If It Feels Right … ."

[16] David Brooks, *Road to Character* (New York: Random House, 2015).

[17] Jean Piaget, "Intellectual Evolution from Adolescence to Adulthood," *Human Development* 15 (1972).

[18] Daniel Kahneman, *Thinking, Fast and Slow* (Toronto: Anchor Canada, 2013).

[19] David Brooks, *Road to Character*.

[20] Antonio Demagio, "Part IV: Long After Consciousness," *Self Comes to Mind* (New York: Vintage, 2012).

[21] Baier, Kurt, *The Moral Point of View*.

[22] Leon Festinger, *A Theory of Cognitive Dissonance* (Stanford: Stanford University Press, 1957).

[23] David Brooks, *Road to Character*. (15).

Part I: Thinking through moral dilemmas in pursuit of justice or fairness

Chapter 1: Challenge

[24] David Brooks, *Road to Character*

[25] David Brooks, "If It Feels Right … ."

[26] Ibid.

[27] Ibid.

[28] Justin Pritchard. "Google Driverless Car Sideswipes Bus, Gets Caught On Video." Toronto: Huffington Post. The Associated Press reported in THE CANADIAN PRESS. (March 10, 2016). http://www.huffingtonpost.ca/2016/03/10/google-driverless-car-bus-accident-video_n_9426134.html.

[29] Jacob Bogage, "Tesla driver using autopilot killed in crash," *The Washington Post*, June 20, 2016.

Chapter 2: Cognitive development

[30] Jonathan Haidt, *The Righteous Mind*. (New York: Vintage Books, 2012).

[31] Jean Piaget, "Intellectual Evolution from Adolescence to Adulthood," *Human Development*, Vol. 15, No. 1, 1972.

[32] Lawrence Kohlberg and Rochelle Mayer, "Development as the Aim of Education," *Harvard Educational Review*, 42, no.4 (1972). For a critique of Kohlberg's view, read Carol Gilligan, *In a Different Voice* (Cambridge: Harvard University Press, 1982). For an alternative view, see Antonio Demagio, "Part IV: Long After Consciousness," in *Self Comes to Mind* (New York: Vintage, 2012) 203-315.

[33] Lawrence Kohlberg and Rochelle Mayer, "Development as the Aim of Education," *Harvard Educational Review*,

[34] Leon Festinger, *A Theory of Cognitive Dissonance*.

[35] Lawrence Kohlberg and Rochelle Mayer, "Development as the Aim of Education," *Harvard Educational Review*,

[36] Otto B. Toews, *Youth, Law and Morality: A Program in Moral and Legal Education*. (Masters thesis, University of Manitoba,69).

[37] Ibid. (70)

[38] Ibid. (78)

[39] Jeremy Rifkin, *The Empathic Civilization* (New York: Jeremy P. Tarcher/ Penguin, 2009), 153.

[40] IBID 27

Chapter 3: Effortful Reasoning

[41] Daniel Kahneman, *Thinking, Fast and Slow*.

[42] Ibid.

[43] Richard Cohen, *Miley Cyrus, Steubenville and teen culture run amok*, Washington Post, September 2, 2013.

[44] Ibid.

[45] Ibid.

[46] Antonio Demagio, *Self Comes to Mind*.

Chapter 4: Principles Thinking Model

[47] David Brooks, *Road to Character* (249)

Chapter 5: Duty

[48]These concepts are developed in Otto, B. Toews, *Discretion and Justice in Educational Administration: Towards a Normative Conceptual Framework.* PhD diss., University of Manitoba, 1981, 123-134.

[49] David Brooks, *Road to Character* 244

[50] Ibid. (246)

[51] Ibid. (249)

[52] Ibid. (249)

[53] Ibid.

[54] Ibid.

[55] Ibid. (259)

[56] Ibid. (249)

[57] Ibid.

[58] Ibid. (249)

[59] When I was a Junior High School history teacher, a small group of teachers regularly engaged in spirited discussions at the noon hour whenever our schedules permitted. In addition, six or seven of us would meet regularly twice a month in the evening during the school year to continue our discussions without the interruptions of daily schedules at school. We covered a wide range of topics and books we had read. Frequently, our evening discussions were quite formal reflecting our involvement in graduate programs. The hypothetical conversations in this book reflect these discussions. At that time, we did not call these discussion thought experiments but we explored each other's thoughts in a systematic way.

[60] David Brooks, "If It Feels Right ... ."

Chapter 6: Rights

[61] The Conceptual Framework for *Rights* is drawn from Toews, Otto, B., *Discretion and Justice in Educational Administration: Towards a Normative Conceptual Framework.* Ph, D. diss., University of Manitoba, 1981, 135 – 148.

[62] Brooks quotes Rabbi Joseph Soloveitchik in *Lonely Man of Faith* in *Road to Character* (xi)

[63] David Brooks, *Road to Character.* (xii)

[64] David Brooks, *Road to Character.* (171)

65 David Brooks, *Road to Character*. (247)

66 David Brooks, *Road to Character*. (246)

67 David Brooks *Road to Character*. (246)

68 David Brooks *Road to Character*. (248)

69 David Brooks refers to Dr. Seuss's 1990 book *Oh, the Places You'll Go!* (252)

70 Ibid.

71 David Brooks quotes, Charles Taylor a philosopher, in *Road to Character* (249)

72 Ibid.

73 David Brooks quotes celebrity chef Mario Batali in *Road to Character* (7)

Chapter 7: Motive

74 The Conceptual Framework for Motive is drawn from Otto B. Toews, *Discretion and Justice in Educational Administration: Towards a Normative Conceptual Framework*. PhD Diss., University of Manitoba, 1981, 149 – 167.

75 Lawrence Kohlberg and Rochelle Mayer, "Development as the Aim of Education."

76 David Brooks *Road to Character*. (21)

77 David Brooks *Road to Character*. (249)

78 Ibid.

79 Ibid.

80 David Brooks, " If It Feels Right ..."

81 David Brooks *Road to Character*. (250)

Chapter 8: Desert

82 The Conceptual Framework for Desert is drawn from Otto B. Toews, *Discretion and Justice in Educational Administration: Towards a Normative Conceptual Framework*, PhD Diss., University of Manitoba, 1981, (168 – 176).

83 Otto B. Toews, "Sponsor a Village", last modified 2016, http://www.sponsoravillage.ca

84 Adapted from "The greatest grudge match: France versus Ireland," *Globe and Mail*, Nov. 19, 2009.

85 David Brooks, " If It Feels Right ..."

86 David Brooks, *Road to Character*.

[87] David Brooks, *Road to Character.* (21)

[88] Ibid

[89] David Brooks, *Road to Character.* (171)

[90] David Brooks, *Road to Character.* (115)

[91] David Brooks, " If It Feels Right ..."

[92] David Brooks, *Road to Character.* (67)

[93] Steve Pinker, *The Better Angels of Our Nature: Why Violence Has Declined,* (New York: Penguin Books, 2011). (526)

[94] Steve Pinker, *The Better Angels of Our Nature: Why Violence Has Declined.* (538)

Chapter 9: Justice

[95] The Conceptual Framework for Justice is drawn from Otto B. Toews, *Discretion and Justice in Educational Administration: Towards a Normative Conceptual Framework*, PHD Diss., University of Manitoba, 1981, 177 – 190.

[96] Daniel Kahneman, *Thinking, Fast and Slow* (Toronto: Anchor Canada, 2013).

[97] David Brooks, *Road to Character* .(247)

[98] Steve Pinker, *The Better Angels of Our Nature: Why Violence Has Declined,* (538)

[99] John Rawls, *A Theory of Justice,* (Cambridge: Harvard University Press, 1973), (80)

Part II Resolving moral dilemmas in pursuit of justice requires a sense of empathy or fellow feeling

[100] David Hume, *Treatise of Human Nature* (Dover Publication, London, 1738)

[101] John Rawls, *Theory of Justice.*

[102] Nel Nodding, *Caring* (Berkeley: University of California Press, 1084)

[103] Carol Gilligan, *In a Different Voice* (Cambridge: Harvard University Press, 1982)

Chapter 10: Cognition and the Affect

[1004] David Hume, *Treatise of Human Nature.*

[105] Ibid

[106] John Rawls, *Theory of Justice.*

[107] John Rawls, *Theory of Justice.* 75

[108] Nel Nodding, *Caring*

[109] Nel Nodding, *Caring* 78

[110] Carol Gilligan, *In a Different Voice.*

[111] Carol Gilligan, *In a Different Voice.* 174

[112] Antonio Damagio, *Self Comes to Mind,* (Vintage: New York, 2012). For additional insights on what neuroscientists have to say about the development of the brain, read, Mario Beauregard, *brain wars* (Toronto: Harper Collins, 2012); Daniel Bor, *Ravenous Brain* (New York: Basic Books, 2012). For additional readings on what psychologists recently have to say about the brain and the mind consider the following: Michael Shermer, *The Believing Brain,* (Henry Holt and Company, New York, 2011); Norman Doidge, *The Brain that Changes Itself* (New York: Penguin Books 2007); Jonathon Haidt, *The Righteous Mind* (New York: Vintage Books, 2012); Bruce Hood, 2013. *The Self Illusion: How the Social Brain Creates Identity* (Toronto: Harper-Collins, 2013). General readings include John Brockman, *Thinking* (New York: Harper-Collins, 2013); Ray Kurzweil, *Singularity is Near* (London: Penguin Books 2005) and *How to Create a Mind* (London: Penguin Books, 2012); Robert Martin, *The Opposable Mind* (Boston: Harvard Business Press, 2009); Michael Shermer, 2011 *The Believing Brain* (New York: Henry Holt and Company, 2011) and *The Moral Arc* (New York: Henry Holt and Company, 2015); Paul Thagard, *The Brain and the Meaning of Life* (New Jersey: Princeton University Press, 2010; Clive Thompson, *Smarter Than You Think* (New York: The Penguin Press, 2013); Matte, Gabor, *When the Body Says No* (Toronto: Vintage Canada, 2003); Matt Ridley, *The Rational Optimist* (New York: Harper-Collins, 2010); and Joshua Greene, *Moral Tribes* (New York: The Penguin Press,2013).

[113] Antonio Damagio, *Self Comes to Mind,*

[114] Ibid

[115] Jeremy Rifkin, *The Empathic Civilization* (146)

[116] David Brooks, *Road to Character*

Chapter 11: Moral Values Principle Tests

[117] Kurt Baier in *A Moral Point of View.*

[118] Daniel Kahneman, *Thinking, Fast and Slow.*

Chapter 12: Dissonance

[119] (Leon Festinger, *A Theory of Cognitive Dissonance*, (14)

[120] Ibid.

[121] Ibid. (13)

[122] Ibid. (271)

[123] Ibid.

Part III: Application of the Principled Thinking Model and the Moral Values Principle Tests

Chapter 13: Censoring Internet Access

[124] Censoring Internet Access is based on an interview with the author by a radio reporter in the 1990's.

Chapter 14: Irate parent

[125] Irate Parent is a hypothetical scenario written by the author. For an actual Case Study on the removal of the novel, *Of Mice and Men* by John Steinbach, go to Otto B. Toews, *Discretion and Justice in Educational Administration: Towards a Normative Conceptual Framework* (257-311).

Chapter 15: Considerate parent

[126] A hypothetical scenario written by the author.

[127] Daniel Kahneman, *Thinking, Fast and Slow* (13)

Chapter 16: Arthur's Moral Dilemma

[128] A hypothetical scenario written by the author.

Chapter 17: Cyber Bullying

[129] "11 Facts about Cyber Bullying," Dosomething.org. https://www.dosomething.org/us/facts/11-facts-about-cyber-bullying.

Chapter 18: Civil Society

[130] Jeremy Rifkin is a senior lecturer at the Wharton School's Executive Education Program at the University of Pennsylvania where he instructs CEO's and corporate management on new trends in science, technology, the economy, and society.

[131] Ibid.

Chapter 19: International Responsibilities

[132] Otto B. Toews, "Room to Read and Write," Sponsor A Village www.sponsoravillage.ca, last in 2016.

Chapter 20: The Enemy is Neglect of Mental Illness

[133] Mitchell Anderson, "The Enemy Is Neglect of Mental Illness" (*TheTyee.ca*, October 25, 2014)

Chapter 21: Reconciliation

[134] "A history of residential schools in Canada" CBC NEWS (Mar 21, 2016). http://www.cbc.ca/news/canada/a-history-of-residential-schools-in-canada-1.702280

[135] *Truth and Reconciliation.* (Winnipeg: Truth and Reconciliation Commission of Canada, 2015).

[136] "Residential school survivors share their stories at Truth and Reconciliation event in Vancouver" by Yolande Cole. Straight (September 21, 2013). http://www.straight.com/news/428331/residential-school-survivors-share-their-stories-truth-and-reconciliation-event-vancouver.

Part III: What if ...

[137] A hypothetical scenario written by the author. It is based on possible futures generated by Ray Kurzweil in *Singularity is Near: When Humans Transcend Biology*, 2005 and Yuval Noah Harari in *Homo Deus: A Brief History of Tomorrow*, 2015.

[138] Ray Kurzweil in *Singularity is Near: When Humans Transcend Biology*.

[139] See reference to Stephen Hawkings in Alex Mason "Stephen Hawking's warning on artificial intelligence long way off," CBC News (December 4, 2014)

[140] See reference to Darren Abramson in Alex Mason, "Stephen Hawking's warning on artificial intelligence long way off."